3-3-12

message of your
Life! Live it,
Breathe it, He
Will Reveal it
to you deeper &
deeper & more &
more! You
shine as
Jesus in His
Lizzie suit
pours forth
from you every
second of your
day!
    I love You,
     Melody

MYSTICAL UNION

by JOHN CROWDER

Sons of Thunder Ministries & Publications
Santa Cruz, CAlifornia

MYSTICAL UNION by John Crowder
Published by Sons of Thunder Ministries & Publications
P.O. Box 3591
Santa Cruz, CA 95063

www.thenewmystics.com
Phone: **1-877-343-3245**
Email: info@thenewmystics.org

Library of Congress Catalog Number: 2010915409
International Standard Book Number: 097708261X

Printed in the United States of America

9 8 7 6 5 4 3

Χριστῷ συνεσταύρωμαι ζῶ δὲ οὐκέτι ἐγώ ζῇ δὲ ἐν ἐμοὶ
Χριστός ὃ δὲ νῦν ζῶ ἐν σαρκί ἐν πίστει ζῶ τῇ τοῦ υἱοῦ τοῦ
θεοῦ τοῦ ἀγαπήσαντός με καὶ παραδόντος ἑαυτὸν ὑπὲρ
ἐμοῦ

I have been co-crucified with Christ and I no longer
live, but Christ lives in me. The life I live in the body, I
live by faith in the Son of God, who loved me and gave
Himself for me.

Galatians 2:20

DEDICATION & ACKNOWLEDGEMENTS

This book is dedicated to Benjamin Dunn – a friend and co-laborer in the glorious gospel of grace. I can hardly take credit for anything you're about to read. The themes and ideas here were pioneered collectively through years of traveling, teaching and revelating together. I highly recommend his book, *The Happy Gospel*, as a fitting companion to this volume.

Thanks also to Georgian and Winnie Banov for their joyful and tireless work in unpacking Romans 6. I am so glad you forgot about everything else.

Thanks to all of our partners, friends and supporters around the world who are fueling the reformation at hand. Your willingness to run with the radical scandal of the cross is ushering in an ecstatic movement to the Body of Christ and the world. You are making history.

And thanks to our enemies. You confirm us in who we are. You teach us to forgive. You strengthen our conviction to never leap off this crazy tilt-a-whirl of grace. Longfellow once wrote, "If we could read the secret history of our enemies, we should find in each man's life, sorrow and suffering enough to disarm all hostility."

Above all, I am grateful for a happy, loving and extraordinarily adventurous family. My wife Lily and our four children continually ride the waves of ministry life. Driving cross-country, flying around the globe – doing home school in the back of an SUV. Yet we don't consider ourselves to have yet done an honest day's work so far. For us, life is about the *play*. That's the sound of the homeward call. Robert Capon once wrote of ministry, "If you can't figure out a way of doing it for fun, do yourself and everybody else a favor and don't do it."

CONTENTS

AUTHOR'S NOTE

When you think of the cross, do you think of *fun*?

If the answer is "no" then you have not been taught the cross aright.

There is a delicious feast prepared for the believer. Nothing is more satisfying than the revelation of what Christ has conclusively accomplished for you. This book threatens to turn your Christianity upside down. No longer a struggle to please God – the Truth plunges you into a celebration of what *He has done for you*.

It is high time the church gets delivered from *God pleasing*. As the apostle Paul said, "Convinced that no human being can please God by self-improvement, we believed in Jesus as the Messiah so that we might be set right before God by trusting in the Messiah, not by trying to be good" (Gal. 2:16, MSG).

Does happy, effortless Christianity sound scandalous to you? Does a daily walk of joyful, sinless existence seem like an impossibility?

If the answer is "yes" then allow me to introduce you to *the gospel*. At least the gospel as you may have never heard it before. The *original version* is so easy and pleasurable that it's offensive.

There is a reason that the gospel was first called "good news." It is a gloriously happy message of effortless union with God. It comes as an utter shock and outrage to the depressive human willpower that is common to religion.

9

AUTHOR'S NOTE

I want to warn you here from the start that much of your existing theology is going to be <u>flushed</u> <u>down</u> <u>the</u> toilet as you read. Areas where you assumed to be an expert on the "basics" of the faith may prove to be areas of borderline apostasy in your theological suitcase.

I want to en-*courage* you to take courage. It takes a brave person to allow their world to be flipped on its head. We will barbecue some sacred theological cows. Yum! At times, it could be a virtual slaughterhouse. And perhaps you'll find that you've believed some things incorrectly – maybe even built a ministry machine on a bad foundation – for the past 20 years. The best approach is not to get angry. Consider the bright side ... *that's better than 21.*

Let everything you knew about the cross of Christ be revolutionized as you read. Allow your mind to be changed. May you comprehend the unforced rhythms of grace.

INTRODUCTION:
A REFORMED MYSTIC

The gospel is a mystical message.

From the onset, you may want an explanation of that word – *mystical*. And just to be honest, if you've been a professional pew warmer for any amount of time, you may be a bit squeamish about the title of this book. You may simply be asking: *What is mysticism?*

In our present day, unless you are a scholar, seminarian or church historian, chances are that you think the word "mystical" applies to the occult, new age or some other deviant spiritual practice. The term "mysticism" is wrongly used to describe anything under the sun that is deemed spiritual or enlightening. Writer Jerald C. Brauer rightly notes the vague usage of the word. He says, "The term has been applied to everything from wild antinomian ecstasies to extreme quietism. It has been used to describe any longing of the soul for God, any first hand religious experience, various theosophical, occult, or magical speculations, or any vague mysterious esoteric systems. Often it has been equated with pantheism, romanticism, idealism, or any system of immanence."

No matter its improper usage. "Mysticism" is a word that started in the church. For centuries, when one spoke of the *mystics*, he referred only to those believers who experienced an interactive life with Christ – full of intimacy and supernatural power. But various non-Christian religious movements have hijacked the word. This is why clarification is needed that we are talking about "Christian mysticism" and not some aberrant form of paganism.

11

INTRODUCTION

Mystical union should not be a foreign concept to the believer, for we are talking about our union with Christ. We are in Him, and He is in us. Mysticism is an *experience* of this union with God. And the union is procured by Christ's atoning sacrifice.

I define mysticism as: *an experience of union with God – a consciousness of the reality of God. The belief that the reality of God can be infused through subjective experience.* Christians experience God directly through our belief in Jesus Christ, enabling us to apprehend spiritual truths that are inaccessible through intellectual means.

The apostle Paul was the church's first mystical theologian. He used the Greek word "mysterion" twenty-one times out of the total twenty-seven usages in the New Testament.[1] Paul almost always used the word in the sense that the mystery has already been *revealed*. Are you hungry to see the mysteries of God revealed? Let me clue you into the spoiler. Right here in the introduction of the book, I will reveal the plot twist that the whole Bible hinges upon. I am going to tell you the "the mystic secret of God." Buckle up and hold onto your seats ... here it comes ...

Paul says we should "become progressively more intimately acquainted with and may know more definitely and accurately and thoroughly that **mystic secret of God, [which is] Christ** (the Anointed One)" (Col. 2:2, AMP).

There it is! Christ is the *mystic secret of God*. Sorry if you were looking for something else. If you're looking

---

[1] *Dictionary of Paul and His Letters*, edited by Gerald Hawthorne, Ralph Martin and Daniel Reid (Downers Grove, IL: InterVarsity Press, 1993), 622.

INTRODUCTION

for a "deeper" revelation than Christ, you have picked up the wrong book.

All of God has been plainly published in Christ. "Even the mystery which hath been hid from ages and from generations, but now is made manifest to His saints ... which is Christ in you, the hope of Glory" (Col. 1:26, 27, KJV).

Like Paul, you are now called to be a "dispenser of the mysteries of God" by sharing the glorious good news of the gospel (1 Cor. 4:1). The gospel is an utterly supernatural message. It is otherworldly. It is not a human message.

Now allow me to make a brief apology ...

There are a number of you who are already well acquainted with Christian mysticism. If you are expecting this volume to guide you through the caverns of the soul like Theresa of Avila or ascend the seven-story mountain with Thomas Merton, you will be sorely disappointed. Ruysbroeck, John of the Cross and the usual suspects do not reflect the same type of mysticism we are advocating.

We are not climbing an unseen ladder. We have already arrived.

I need the delicious ecstasies, experiences and the practice of God's presence that I find in the historic catholic mystics. But I also need the simple faith of the reformers.

In reading most of the traditional mystics, one would think that union with God comes after a long process of 50 years of prayer and fasting. I am a *reformed* mystic. I believe that my union with God happened 2,000 years

13

A REFORMED MYSTIC

ago on the cross of Christ. It is completely independent and even opposed to my own efforts to procure it.

Perhaps you are familiar with my first book, *The New Mystics.* I have long made the case for a renaissance of a *new kind of mysticism.* This new mysticism relishes the intimacy and supernatural experience of the saints. I embrace even the wildest miracles of the mystics – from floating off the ground to walking through walls. But my union with God is completely founded on the finished work of *Christ's cross.* The world has never seen a mysticism that is utterly supernatural, and yet thoroughly effortless and grace-based.

Often, the leaders of the reformation were thought to be at odds with the church mystics. The reformers were about simple faith. The mystics were about experience. I make the case that reformation and mysticism are not mutually exclusive. Rather, the faith approach of the reformers should be the true gateway into the supernatural heights of mystical experience.

Much of traditional mysticism has been marked by a thinly veiled "works" righteousness. Herein lies the difference in the old and new mysticism. Traditionally, it was implied – though not overtly stated – that mystical union with God was attained not strictly by grace but by our own spiritual jumping jacks. This is a thinly veiled suggestion – no one would come outright and say it that way. Instead, they talk about *yielding,* or *surrendering* or *overcoming self.* Its focus was often on ascetic practice, prayer and annihilation of self through meditation or other means to gain reception into God. Such self-effort to eradicate self consists of what reformation scholar Wilhelm Kolfhaus called "an unmediated communion with God."[2] What does that mean? It means your relationship with God is not based on a Mediator, but instead, you are relying on your own spiritual disciplines. Here, the grace of Christ is bypassed.

Let us not drag up any vestiges of *that* kind of mysticism. In fact, the point of this book is to help you renounce all your own endeavors to find favor with your Father.

For sure, the mystics of the church truly loved Jesus. I believe that the Lord blessed them with miracles and fantastic experiences because He is gracious. But not because they impressed Him with their prayer and fasting. He moved in many of their lives not because of their theology, but *in spite of it*. I can glean from their experiences. But I can unflinchingly toss out the formulas they offer to get what they've got.

We now have five hundred years of grace theology under our belt, to know that mystical union with God is not achieved by our own effort. It happened in one fell swoop on the cross of Christ.

Just as ascetic disciplines do not bring us into union, neither do experiences themselves. Many mystics taught that union itself was an experience. But I am teaching that we can experience the union we already have.

Ecstatic encounters and visions do not make us one with Christ. However, faith in the work of the cross does. Trusting in Christ's work can and should produce

---

[2] Wilhelm Kolfhaus, *Christusgemeinschaft bei Johannes Calvin*, 126. Translated by Dennis Tamburello, *Union with Christ* (Louisville: Westminster John Knox Press, 1994), 5.

all manner of supernatural manifestations. Union itself is not a subjective experience that is attained by our interior efforts. Does union *produce* subjective or "felt" experiences? Yes! But the union is not dependent on those experiences, anymore than it is attained by human effort.

I do not mean to suggest that all of the historical mystics *rejected* faith as their ultimate connector to God. Trust in Christ's finished work was paramount to them all. But as a whole, it is safe to say there was a lack of revelation of the gospel of grace.

I want to be fair with my criticism. On the reformers' end, they had a great grasp of faith – however, they tended to get more cerebral than experiential. It is easy to slip into a Greco-rationalistic, reason-based approach to God. Faith is not of the *mind*, it is of the *heart*. To the credit of the mystics, theirs was a life and language of love.

Did you know that – despite their criticism of the mystics – the Protestant reformers did indeed have a concept of mystical union? Even John Calvin used the term *mystical union* verbatim. Consider Calvin's statement:

Therefore, that joining together of the Head and members, that indwelling of Christ in our hearts – in short, that mystical union – are accorded by us the highest degree of importance, so that Christ, having been made ours, makes us sharers with Him in the gifts with which He has been endowed.[3] BAM!

---

[3] John Calvin, *Institutes of the Christian Religion*, 3.11.10. Referenced in Tamburello, *Union with Christ*, 84.

In addition, Martin Luther had an appreciation and understanding of our union with God. Only it was *faith-based*, and rightly did not hinge on spiritual disciplines.

"The core meaning of 'mysticism' is union with Christ. Prayer and meditation are the usual means to that end. Since Luther taught that faith is the primary means to union with Christ, it is possible to miss seeing his theology as mystical," writes Eric Swensson[4]

I will add one more constructive criticism to the work of the reformers – *they did not go far enough*. Yes, their theology on faith was revolutionary. But they missed it on the topic of *indwelling sin* in a believer. This is where the puritans derailed and took the ship into a downward spiral. The reformation was cut short in many ways. Or perhaps I should say that the reformation *is not yet finished*. This will be a principal focus of this book. Even the reformers were not reformed enough. You will see how the cross united us to Christ, not just positionally, but effectively. It doesn't just cover our sins, but eradicates sinfulness itself from us.

Just as there is a *new mysticism* on the rise, I believe it is coupled with a new reformation. The good news will be preached with such clarity that, even the days of Luther will seem utterly primitive in its concepts of grace and faith.

In conclusion, what I am saying is that the mystics and reformers both needed one another. The mystics needed the reformers' faith. The reformers rejected the mystics' experience.

---

[4] Eric Jonas Swensson, "Luther's Mystical Theology" (2005), http://www.pubtheo.com/page.asp?pid=1436 (accessed June 18, 2010).

INTRODUCTION

We need to be more experiential than the mystics, and more reformed than the reformers. This will only happen through a radical embrace of the scandal of the cross.

I hope that this book challenges you. I hope it provokes you. It is not intended to provoke you to *frustration* – but rather to childlike joy and trust in Christ's cross. It is a short book with a vicious little bite at times. But there is plenty of sugar to help the medicine go down.

May the cross of Christ be as sweet water to your soul. May you be awakened to the bliss of the crucified One who has taken up permanent residence in your heart.

John Crowder

TRANSLATION INDEX

In the following chapters, we will draw from multiple translations of the scriptures. The author has accumulated upward of 150 versions in English to date, and chosen some of the best here to accurately convey a robust understanding of scripture. A number of these are rare and out of print. We actively encourage you to begin your own translation library for a deeper drink of the pure, undiluted gospel!

An explanation of abbreviations

The translations used in this book can be identified by the following codes:

AAT – *The Holy Bible in the Language of Today: An American Translation* (Philadelphia/New York: A.J. Holman Company, 1976). William F. Beck.

AKJV – *American King James Version* (Public Domain as of 1999). Michael Peter "Stone" Engelbrite.

AMP – *The Amplified Bible* (Grand Rapids: Zondervan Publishing House and The Lockman Foundation, 1954, 1958, 1962, 1964, 1965, 1987). Translated mostly by Frances Siewert.

ASV – *The American Standard Version Holy Bible* (Star Bible and Tract Corp., 1901).

BAS – *The New Testament in Basic English* (New York: Cambridge University Press, 1941).

BCJ – *The Heart of Paul: A Relational Paraphrase of the New Testament* (Waco, TX: Word Books, 1976). Ben Campbell Johnson.

BER – *Berkeley Version of the New Testament From the Original Greek With Brief Footnotes* (Berkeley: James J. Gillick and Co., 1945). Verkuyl Gerrit.

BNT – *The New Testament: A Translation by William Barclay* (London: Arthur James Ltd., 1968, 1969, 1988). William Barclay.

19

CAS – *God's New Covenant: A New Testament Translation* (Grand Rapids: William B. Eerdmans Publishing Co., 1989). Heinz Cassirer.

CJB – *Complete Jewish Bible* (Clarksville, MD: Jewish New Testament Publications, Inc., 1998). David Stern.

CON – *The Life and Epistles of St. Paul* (Grand Rapids: William B. Eerdmans Publishing Co., 1978). W.J. Conybeare, J.S. Howson.

COR – *St. Paul from the Trenches* (Boston: Houghton Mifflin Co., 1938). Gerald Warre Cornish.

CPG – *The Cotton Patch Version of Paul's Epistles* (Piscataway, NJ: New Century Publishers, 1968). Clarence Jordan.

DIS – *The Distilled Bible: New Testament* (Stone Mountain, GA: P. Benjamin Publishers, 1980). Roy Greenhill.

DRB – *Douay-Rheims Bible 1582-1609* (Fitzwilliam, NH: Loreto Publications, 2007).

ECK – *The Sermon on the Mount,* (Passage adaptation accessible at http://www.corneroak.com/sermon_lyrics.html). Lindsey Eck.

ESV – *The English Standard Version Bible: Containing the Old and New Testaments with Apocrypha* (Oxford: Oxford University Press, 2009).

GBS – *The Epistles of Paul in Modern English* (Wheaton, IL: Verploegh Editions, 1980 ed.). George Barker Stevens.

GSPD – *The New Testament, An American Translation* (Chicago: University of Chicago Press, 1923). Edgar J. Goodspeed.

GWT – *God's Word Translation* (Holiday, FL: Green Key Books, 1995, 2003).

KJV – *The Holy Bible King James Version: 1611 Edition.*

KNOX – *The New Testament of our Lord and Saviour Jesus Christ* (Springfield: Templegate Publishers, 1945). Ronald A. Knox.

LNT – *The New Testament* (New York: North Point Press, 1996). Richmond Lattimore.

MIR – *Mirror Translation* (Visit www.mirrorreflection.net). Francois du Toit.

MOF – *The Bible: James Moffatt Translation* (San Francisco: Harper Collins, 1922/1994). James Moffatt.

MON – *The New Testament in Modern English* (Valley Forge: Judson Press, 1924). Helen Barrett Montgomery.

MSG – *The Message* (Colorado Springs: NavPress Publishing Group, 2005 ed.). Eugene Peterson.

NASB – *New American Standard Bible* (La Habra, Ca.: The Lockman Foundation, 1977, 1995).

NCV – *The Holy Bible, New Century Version* (Nashville: Word Publishing, 1987, 1988, 1991).

NEB – *The New English Bible: New Testament* (New York: Oxford University Press and Cambridge University Press, 1961).

NIV – *The Holy Bible, New International Version* (Grand Rapids: The Zondervan Corporation, 1973, 1978, 1984). International Bible Society.

NKJV – *New King James Version* (Thomas Nelson Publishers, 1982).

NLT – *New Living Translation* (Wheaton: Tyndale House Publishers, 1996, 2004, 2007).

NOR – *The Simplified New Testament* (Grand Rapids: Zondervan Publishing House, 1961). Olaf Norlie.

PHI – *The New Testament in Modern English* (New York: The Macmillan Co., 1962). J.B. Phillips.

RSV – *The Holy Bible Revised Standard Version* (New York: Thomas Nelson & Sons, 1952).

SWANN – *New Testament of our Lord and Saviour Jesus Christ* (Robards, KY: George Swann Company, 1947). George Swann.

TAY – *Living Letters: The Paraphrased Epistles* (Wheaton: Tyndale House Publishers, 1962). Kenneth Taylor.

TCNT – *The Twentieth Century New Testament* (New York/Chicago/Toronto: Fleming H. Revell Company).

TJB – *The Jerusalem Bible* (London: Darton, Longman & Todd, 1966).

TLB – *The Living Bible* (Wheaton: Tyndale House Publishers, 1971, 1979).

TNT – *The New Translation: The Letters of the New Testament* (Tyndale House Publishers and The Society for The New Translation).

WAND – *The New Testament Letters* (New York: Oxford University Press, 1950). J.W.C. Wand.

WAY – *The Letters of Saint Paul* (Chicago: Moody Press, 1950). Arthur S. Way.

WET – *The New Testament: An Expanded Translation* (Grand Rapids: William B. Eerdmans Publishing Co., 1961). Kenneth Wuest.

WEY – *The New Testament in Modern Speech* (New York: Harper and Row Publishers, Inc., 1903). Richard Francis Weymouth.

WMS – *The New Testament: A Translation in the Language of the People* (Chicago: Moody Press, 1963). Charles B. Williams.

WPE – The New Testament: A New Translation in Plain English (Grand Rapids: William B. Eerdmans Publishing Co., 1963). Charles K. Williams.

The author has emphasized some scripture texts in bold lettering. Verses listed without translation references are partially quoted or inferred.

Part 1 ... THE MYTH OF THE FLESH

Your union with God in Christ is instant and effortless. It happened on the cross and was realized the first moment you believed. It is from this vantage point of being "in Christ" that all other doctrines of the church must be built.

A perspective of union will drastically alter your outlook on healing, the miraculous, prayer, fasting and every dimension of your Christianity. Union with God is a simple but revolutionary concept. While you think you may grasp it, I warn you that the following chapters could deeply and irrevocably rattle all of your theological foundations.

A real and vital oneness with God was achieved and *completed* on Christ's cross. Nothing was left undone. This is the foundational principle of the New Testament and the chief thrust of the Pauline epistles. Cambridge Dean C.T. Wood wrote of Paul, "We must insist again that union with the ever-present Christ is the pivot of his religion, and therefore of his theology."[5]

Sounds basic enough, eh? Two becoming one. But hold on ...

There is a two-thousand-year-old heresy that has afflicted the church. Commonly accepted, it is preached like Captain Crunch Sunday morning breakfast cereal from pulpits all over the world. It is the backbone, nerve center and theological foundation for the *religious spirit*.

---

[5] C.T. Wood, *The Life, Letters and Religion of St. Paul* (Edinburgh: T & T Clark, 1925, 1956), 73.

It has made the gospel a non-gospel. It has exchanged the Good News for a "do-it-yourself" morality program. It complicates the simplicity of childlike faith.

But a clarity is coming to the preaching of the gospel that has not been heard since the days of the Apostle Paul. It brings with it a revolutionary change in language and understanding. A movement is underfoot in which the gospel is being rightly articulated. For when the gospel is not being preached in a language the people understand it is time for a reformation.

The truth will set you free.

Here is the heresy of which I speak. Here is the myth that keeps men duped and toiling in the quagmire of their own efforts. The heresy is this: it is the idea that you, as a believer, still have a *sinful nature*.

To some this may seem a simple omission. To others, this is volatile and incendiary speech. It poses severe danger to a lifelong accumulation of systematic self-help doctrines, therapy tactics, inner healing mechanics and innumerable methods and ministry goals that have been built like castles in the sand. It represents the tide coming in to wash it all away.

No sinful nature. Are these wild words? Is this Biblical? What are the implications?

The gospel invalidates every ministry aimed at improving people. God didn't come to fix anybody. He came to kill them and resurrect them from the dead.

If you have been in church for more than a week, you were likely taught that your entire life is a struggle to overcome your fleshly desires, battle off temptation, and somehow to wrestle down and overcome your "old man.'" In the following chapters, we are going to open up our Bibles, dispel the myth, and prove this to be the biggest crock of baloney in Christendom. The results are going to be thrilling, exhilarating, liberating! You are going to plunge into the pleasures of a strong and secure union with God that has been forever purchased, secured and confirmed at no cost to yourself.

This is a book designed to challenge the believer. But the challenge is a sweet one. You will be provoked to an indescribable, delectable joy that can be contained in no other message. You will be challenged to stop striving to get closer to God. You will be encouraged to accept and enjoy the complete and ultimate spiritual union that you already received as a gift of salvation. A gift that you received the very first time you glanced at Love hanging on a tree. No longer will you be plagued with the nagging pressure to annihilate something that doesn't exist. The old, sinful self, which once hindered you from God, has been eradicated once and for all. The *new you* is in perfect cohesion with Him. You are a Siamese twin with Jesus!

Your Ears will be Circumcised

This will be a dangerous book for you. The gospel is a *scandal*. It is an equal opportunity offender both for charismatic and mainline churchgoer alike. You won't be able to stomach the same sermons you once listened to. Some of your favorite preachers won't be your favorite preachers after you hear this message. You'll be ruined. You will begin to filter the things you hear through the lens of the glorious good news. You'll recognize the pseudo-gospel when you hear it. Your ears will perk up. You will be amazed at the overwhelming contradictions that are preached in opposition to the New Testament, both from prophets and seminarians alike.

Because we are going to talk about the *gospel* and the *cross*, do not for a moment think that this is just a book on the basics. I don't want to preach the cross. I want to preach it *aright*.

While this book will provide you with some foundational theology, it is not merely the "milk" while neglecting the "meat." I guarantee that the vast majority of the church needs its theological foundations reformatted in light of the work of the cross. The cross changes everything. If you think the cross is a difficult place, where you are called to suffer and die, you have not been taught the cross aright. The cross is the center and mother lode of all joy and satisfaction, because it is there that your old self has *already died with Christ*. Everything that hindered you from God was eradicated on the cross. Death to your old crooked self was a past-tense occurrence that already took place on *His* cross.

I have been crucified with Christ and I no longer live, but Christ lives in me. The life I live in the body, I live by faith in the Son of God, who loved me and gave Himself for me (Gal. 2:20, NIV).

The work of the cross is not a continual lifelong struggle. Nor is it merely the primary school starting point for the Christian life. It is not just the foundation of the church, but also the ceiling and capstone. The starting line and the finish mark. He is the Alpha and Omega – the Beginning and the End. The first and the last – as well as the creamy center in the middle of it all. Everything in the scriptures points us ultimately to the climactic, grand display of the crucifixion of Christ. It is the center of the universe. Paramount even to the resurrection, if it were possible to compare the two events.

THE MYTH OF THE FLESH

Co-crucified

What is rarely if ever stressed is the reality that you were there with Him on His cross. That your death to self is not a separate one from His, but rather, the two were a concurrent, unified, mystical reality. You were on the tree with Him. You suffered with Him. You died with Him.

Some make the statement, "I was like the good thief hanging next to Jesus. I did some naughty things, but He still saved me." You were not the thief hanging next to Jesus. Your death was much more up-close and personal than that. You were mystically *in Christ*, hanging on *His tree* when He died. The same nail that went through His hands went through yours.

Your complete merger with God took place on the cross, and thanks to that work, you are now an inseparable entity with Him. Your own efforts to achieve this unity are unnecessary. Prayers and supplications to that effect are in vain, because the act is done and accomplished. In fact, your efforts to achieve union are a despicable reproach that can alienate you from grace. *Wow!* Your attempt to approaching God on your own is the "self-righteousness" of which Christ and the apostles warn us about. The very thing that makes you a Christian is your acceptance of *His* perfect sacrifice as the unitive bond between God and man. Being a Christian is not about trying to re-achieve or even further that eternal, inexhaustible union. His perfect sacrifice accomplished a perfect bond.

The Mystical Death

Your union with Christ is as absolute as death itself, because you were somehow a participant in His death on the cross. But it goes a bit deeper. The very thing that separated you from God – sin itself – was evaporated there, as far as you are concerned. God did not just forgive your sins. He destroyed the very governing entity called *sin itself*, which owned and ruled you and made you do naughty things. The propensity for separation from God died once and for all.

Understand that "sin" is not an *action*. The word sin is actually *hamartia* in the Greek. It is an *inward element* that produces evil acts.[6] As the scriptures say, "We know that our old self was put to death on the execution-stake with Him, so that the entire body of our sinful propensities might be destroyed. ..." (Rom. 6:6, CJB).

You were united with Him in a mystical death that took place. The thing that died was your old wicked heart. This is also called the "old man" or the "fleshly nature."

How can we who died to sin still live in it? Do you not know that all of us who have been baptized into Christ Jesus were baptized into His death? (Rom. 6:2-3, ESV)

You "died to sin." This means it is no longer a part of you. You are not a "sinner saved by grace." You are a saint. Take the word *sinner* completely out of the equation now. Grace transformed you from one thing into another. Consider the following translations of the previous verse:

How is it possible for us, such persons as we are, who have been separated once for all from the sinful nature, any longer to live in its grip? (Rom. 6:2, WET)

---

[6] W.E. Vine, *Expository Dictionary of New Testament Words*, 1940 (Accessible online at www.antioch.com.sg/bible/vines).

THE MYTH OF THE FLESH

We died to our old sinful lives, so how can we continue living with sin? (Rom. 6:2, NCV)

God did not just pull you out of sin. He pulled sin out of you! You are now the righteousness of God in Christ Jesus. This is much more than the forgiveness of the old self. This entails the complete *annihilation* of the old self.

God sank the whole ship.

Sin Covered vs. Sin Extracted

He did not just cover His eyes like Santa Clause, pretending He didn't see your naughty behavior, then put you on the "nice list." That's not grace ... that's stupidity. Grace did not just hide God's eyes from your naughty actions – it erased naughtiness itself out of your whole being.

He didn't just give you a pretty screen saver, ignoring all the viruses, porn and spyware on your hard drive. He wiped the whole hard drive out.

The old sinner that you once were completely died to the same degree that Christ completely died. Death to self is not a lifelong process that is dependent on your own efforts. It was a final and complete act. The old you is not still hanging around. Just as you went under the water, so was this a picture of being buried in the ground with Christ. The old you was swallowed up into His death, and the thing that was spit back out was the *new creation* in Christ.

The Living Bible translation says here, "through His death the power of your sinful nature was shattered" (Rom. 6:3, TLB). Also, consider the Williams translation, which says, "Do you not know that all of us who have been *baptized into union* with Christ Jesus have been baptized into His death?" You have been plunged fully into union.

We were therefore **buried** *with Him through baptism into death in order that, just as Christ was raised from the dead through the Glory of the Father, we too may live a new life. If we have been united with Him like this in His death, we will certainly also be united with Him in His resurrection* (Rom. 6:4-5, NIV).

Many people are rightly excited about the resurrection. They want to hurry through all this talk about the cross and get to the after dinner dessert. But if you don't want to think much on the cross, you obviously have a wrong perspective of it. It is a very *appealing* place when you understand it. It is not a place of depression. In fact, it is where all of Heaven opened up and God poured out all your birthdays, Christmases and Disneylands in one fell swoop! It is where every drop of the intoxicating wine of His love was poured out.

The Depressed Self is Dead

You were united with Him in *His* death. What died? The entire fallen personality. Your old depressed self. Your old sinful self. The old fearful you was buried. The old anxious, unbelieving you took a bullet. Your poverty died with Him. Your sickness died with Him. Every bit of darkness and disease that you once were died with Him. All your acne and PMS and road rage took a tumble. Your old religiously sober self was also crucified. The new you is happy, alive and full of the wine of His love! The new you is full of faith. The new, True Self is prosperous, bold and overflowing with life, hope, peace and fruitfulness. The old critical, introverted you is dead. The new self is completely restored to childlike innocence and trust.

Ultimately, the new you is righteous, pure and holy. The old you does not exist any longer. It was an unseen death. You didn't feel the nails, because it was mystical death. But nevertheless, a very real one. You were really present on Calvary. And now, you are a participant in the benefits.

Consider the following translations of the previous verse, Romans 6:5:

We have been planted together (in the ground) in the likeness of His death ... (CON).

We have been united with Him in a death like His ... (RSV).

We have become one with Him by sharing in His death ... (WEY).

When we went under the water, we left the old country of sin behind; when we came up out of the water, we entered into the new country of grace – a new life in a new land! (MSG)

Your old sin-loving nature was buried with Him by baptism when He died ... (TLB).

In the Grave Realm with Christ

Your participation in Christ's death was up close and intimate. It was so vividly personal, that you actually shared a burial with Him. You went into the tomb with Christ. Feel it. Smell the dirt in there. Get this revelation into you. Realize how final it was. You went into the ground with Him. Consider the J.W.C Wand version:

When the water flowed over us it was as if we were in the grave with Him ... (WAND).

Meditate on this reality. I often tell people that if you sit on this chapter of the Bible – Romans 6 – for four years, you will not have wasted a day. In fact, you may end up being the only believer in your neighborhood! These passages give no room for the continued existence of the sinful nature in the life of a believer. Some would mistakenly say, "Yes, the sinful nature died. But then it got back up again." I would ask you for one single verse to back up such a foolish claim. The old nature did not rise up again. The *new you* was resurrected. If you're still sinning, you don't believe that.

The Apostle Paul continues to hammer the point home, adding, "For we know that our *old self was crucified with Him* so that the body of sin might be done away with, that we should no longer be slaves to sin" (Rom. 6:6, NIV). And the Wuest translation continues, "for the one who died once for all stands in the position of a permanent relationship of freedom from the sinful nature" (Rom. 6:7, WET).

✗ *When a man dies, of course, he has finished with sin* (Rom 6:7, TJB). YES! BAM!.

Just as death is a permanent act, so is your union with Christ sealed into a permanent merger. You can truly say, *I am my Beloved's and He is mine* (Song of Sol. 6:3).

God is in a Good Mood

It is imperative that your relationship with God is based on reality. That reality is that all God absorbed all anger and wrath toward sin into Himself on the cross. He destroyed every speck of sin – every ounce of judgment and enmity. The Father was *pleased to bruise* the Son, not because He had bloodlust, but because He was reconciling the nations to Himself (Isa. 53:10).

Of course we give lip service to this truth, but when things are going tough for you in life, do you really trust in this message? Or do you begin to think God must be punishing you because of your poor performance?

God is never looking at your performance as the indicator of His pleasure toward you. So many people live on an emotional rollercoaster ride. They think God is happy with them one day, then disappointed with them another day. It depends on whatever subjective rubber ruler they judge themselves by at the moment. Perhaps you didn't read your Bible enough this week, or lead enough people to Jesus. Oops! You were a little too lazy this week! People tend to judge themselves by all manner of silly criteria like this then project those feelings onto God. If they are having a bad day, they assume God is upset with them. All of this is irrelevant. God is continually looking at one thing, and that is the perfect sacrifice of His Son. Even if you have committed a gross sin, it is acknowledging Christ's mercy toward you that picks you up and moves you forward. Not beating yourself up and trying to change yourself.

How do I Drink the Joy of Union?

You must have a foundation that can handle the immensely incredible weight of joy God has for you. Do you want a joy that is not based on your circumstances? A joy that is not based on your performance? A joy that is not based on the doctor's report, or the bank statement, or whether or not your co-workers like you? There is a joy that is absolutely immune to outward influences. I WANT THAT!

ALL THE TIME!

People email us all the time, and the number one question our ministry ever receives is this, "John, how can I experience the drunken joy of Jesus all the time?" People crave a continual, sustainable joy and fulfillment. They are made for it. But unfortunately, so many people think there is something they must do to get it. Because the church is used to selling formulas, they think there must surely be some "key" they are missing or "process" they must undergo. They think that they must fast or pray a certain way to taste the joy we are experiencing.

Also, since it is so common to make idols of ministers and put them on pedestals, some people just assume we are somehow "specially chosen" or "uniquely anointed" for this gift of joy – yet it will never be accessible to them.

Both of these lines of thought are incorrect. You can't do anything for joy, nor does it belong to the mystical elite. Only God can give you joy in Himself. And that is the whole revelation of the cross.

The Not-So-Secret Source of Joy

Here is the secret source of my joy: *I simply realized that I have been crucified with Christ!* Nothing strange or elusive about it whatsoever! *Everything* that separated me from God (Mr. Pleasure) was abolished once and for all. No matter what I'm feeling at the moment about myself or my circumstances, this single truth trumps it all.

When I wake up everyday, I just know that my old depressed self went into the grave with Jesus. It is difficult for a dead man to be worried about his bank statement or a bad doctor's report. No circumstance can dictate my emotional state. The gospel tells me that <u>my old critically religious self no longer exists</u>! If I'm feeling bored with my Christian walk, the message of the gospel quickly snaps me out of that lie. <u>My old boring self is dead</u>. The new me is intoxicated on the wine of the New Covenant. I can "reckon myself dead" with Christ ... simply realizing that I do not own those negative feelings any longer.

Simply stated: <u>*we drink by faith*</u>! The way <u>you drink the wine of the New Covenant is just to believe it is flowing freely to you right now</u>.

Live by Faith

Stop owning the sinful nature as if it's still hanging around for you to kill. Stop owning fearful, anxious thoughts that belonged to the past. Believe that you are in Christ and that Christ is in you. Negative or sinful feelings can come on strong ... *really* strong! And it is impossible at times to stop them. <u>But that does not mean that you have to *agree* with them or own them.</u> Instead, agree that the old corrupted emotional life died with Christ. Now, you are a recipient of new, resurrected emotions. You are a joint participant in the emotional life of Christ.

You've probably heard it said before from the mouth of some grumpy preacher, "We live by faith, not by feelings!" Often their intent for saying this was to sort of quench your party – as if to say, *don't get too happy.* Maybe you were having too much fun, or getting a little too excited about something ... *settle down! We live by truth, not by feeling!*

What the grumpy preacher said was true, even if his intent was misguided. You live by faith. You live by *truth*, not by feelings. <u>But the truth comes not to kill your buzz, but to enhance it! The *truth* is the dance</u>

BAHAHAHA!

35

floor that holds up the whole party, and Jesus is the life of the party! The truth is that you have been grafted into joy unspeakable and full of Glory. The truth is that your old addicted self was exterminated and doesn't exist anymore. You died a real and verifiable death on Christ's cross. The truth is that everyday for you is a new existence in Heavenly wonderland! Even the worst of external circumstances have no power to quench this factual and internal reality.

The Battle is Over

The truth is that you do not have to kill off or fight those negative emotions or sinful appetites. The truth is that the old appetites have already died. Stop trying to shadowbox something that doesn't exist. Agree with the truth, that you are a new creation. You don't *make yourself* new. Stop striving. Rest in the reality that the old you is dead and powerless. It was nailed to the tree. The new you is enthralled with the pleasures of God. The truth leaves no other option but joy.

Whether you feel it or not, you are now one body and one spirit with Christ. Rest in that reality, and you *will* feel His presence. Faith comes before the feeling. And faith is simply trust. Believe that this mystical death really took place, and you will cease to act like that dead man.

Very simply, the gospel is a revelation that you have died with Him.

The Sinful Nature Abolished

One of the repercussions of this gospel message is that it leaves no more room for active sin in the life of a believer. By making theological room for a sinful nature that no longer exists, religion conveniently gives you a myriad of excuses for bad behavior.

"It's OK ... We're all still sinners." *No, you're not.*

"Well, nobody's perfect." *The Bible says you are.*

"We'll all struggle on this side of Heaven." *You're already seated in Heavenly places.*

"I'm only human." *Not if you're a Christian!*

"Of course, we all sin everyday." *What Bible verse is that? Are you even saved?*

Some would criticize us for preaching what they assume to be *perfection* theology. They would say the gospel is not this simple. That our efforts are still necessary to "kill the flesh" or to *overcome* the old self.

My answer is this: I am not just preaching perfection – I preach *perfect perfection!* This is not the old-school "sinless perfection" theology that the early Wesleyans and the holiness movement preachers advocated. Those guys said it is impossible for a Christian to sin. And a lot of that devolved into do-it-yourself, clean-yourself-up legalism. Nor are we preaching *self-righteousness*. Just the opposite. We are talking about *God-given* righteousness that manifests in an easy, happy, holy life. We're not saying it is "impossible" for a Christian to sin. But we are saying that you don't have to sin another day in your life because you are now completely *evil free*. Living with sin is not your standard. Normative Christianity is sin-free living because you are thoroughly cleansed of evil. You are not a sinner.

Is it Deception to Claim to be Without Sin?

One may ask: can you really claim to be without sin? Doesn't the Bible say that makes you a liar? The Apostle John writes, "If we claim to be without sin, we deceive ourselves and the truth is not in us" (1 John 1:8, NIV). It is always important to put scriptures into context, because this verse is tantamount to 1 John 1:10, only two verses later, where he writes, "If we claim *we have not sinned*, we make Him out to be a liar and His word has no place in our lives" (1 John 1:10, NIV). John is talking about *past tense* sin. Of course we have all sinned at some point. We were born into a fallen world. But Christ has changed that.

John is not saying that believers are *still* sinners. We all acknowledge that we have sinned before at some point in our past. In fact, we all lived a false identity completely possessed and depraved by sin! Know that John is largely focusing his letter toward gnostic heresies – gnostics who denied that they were ever sinners. Without an acknowledgment of sin, there is no hope of conversion for we can never profess a need for a savior. Some gnostics went so far as to say that Christ never suffered, thus repudiating the essential purpose of His coming: *to die for the sins of mankind.*

But now that you have received Christ's death as your own, a supernatural transformation has taken place. Back to your true identity. John doesn't say you're still a sinner. John goes on to tell us in this very same letter that if you go on sinning *you are a child of the devil!* He clearly says that you can't be both a saint and a sinner.

No one who lives in Him keeps on sinning. No one who continues to sin has either seen Him or known Him. Dear children, do not let anyone lead you astray. He who does what is right is right-

*eous, just as He is righteous. **He who does what is sinful is of the devil**, because the devil has been sinning from the beginning. The reason the Son of God appeared was to destroy the devil's work. **No one who is born of God will continue to sin**, because God's seed remains in him; **he cannot go on sinning**, because he has been born of God. This is how we know who the children of God are and who the children of the devil are: **Anyone who does not do what is right is not a child of God**; nor is anyone who does not love his brother* (1 John 3:6, NIV).

Legalistic, do-it-yourself Christians hate this passage, because it indicts them. They get nervous, that if they ever sin, they will become the devil's child! This just proves that they are tense and anxious and trying to maintain their own salvation. John is just making it clear that it is impossible to stop sinning without real conversion! And real conversion effortlessly leads you to a happy, holy life. I absolutely love these verses, because they are proof positive of a real, tangible transformation that only Christ can accomplish. Saved people don't sin.

What a scandal. If you're still not convinced that the cross is the ultimate offense, go to your pastor next Sunday and say, "Hi pastor. I'm perfect." Watch his expression, and notice to see how quickly the disclaimer comes to put a wet blanket on you!

If I'm Not a Sinner, Why do I Still Sin?

And so now, we come to the real meat of the question. This is where the rubber hits the road. The most puzzling question that people ask is this: *If I don't have a sinful nature, why do I still sin?*

Some people see a disparity between what they believe and what their daily lives look like. This very gap
between the scriptures and the reality of their daily lives
is what causes so many theologians and Christian
therapists to contort the word of God and conform it to
their naughty behavior. In other words, they think: *because I still sin, then surely I still have a sinful nature.*
But you never base the truth on your experiences. Instead, your experiences should be dictated by the truth.

We are faith-based mystics.

If you still wrestle with sin as a believer, there are a
couple of options as to why this may be. This question
has a multiple-choice answer.

Question: *If I don't have a sinful nature, why do I still
sin?*

    A) Maybe you're an unbeliever.
    B) Maybe no one ever told you any of this.

For most of you reading this, option A is not true for
you. You're a Christian. Obviously, an unbeliever *does*
still live by the false identity as a *sinner.*

However, it is possible that you never actually heard or
believed the gospel, even though you clocked into
church for decades. Maybe you've attended thousands
of prophecy conferences and deliverance classes, but
still you never heard the message of grace. Maybe you
just thought Christianity was a do-it-yourself morality
club. A clean-yourself-up process of continually seeking but never finding God. If that's you – if you were
never actually transformed by the glorious finished
work of Christ, don't cry over those wasted years.
Here's your chance ... accept your salvation!

If you've been taught that Christianity is a lifelong process of struggling and brokenness, I would invite you to be whole. Give up and let Jesus run your Christianity.

If you are a born-again Christian who struggles with sin, then probably choice B is the real reason for it. *No one ever told you that you are not a sinner anymore.* You were probably told over and over again by pastors and leaders that you still have to fight off your old flesh. And so, for years, you ran around like a dog chasing its tail, trying to fix something that was already fixed. And all you did was amplify a problem that has already been taken care of.

You've been told to expect your whole life to be a struggle against sin. If you think you're still a sinner, then guess what? What do you think your life is going to manifest? C.S. Lewis once said, "You are what you believe." If you believe you are still a sinner, you will manifest sin. If you believe you are the righteousness of God in Christ Jesus, then you are going to manifest righteousness. Believe you are holy and you will manifest holy. That's who you really are.

This is not the so-called power of positive thinking. This is aligning with the word of God.

Trust Your New Identity to Manifest Reality

Faith comes before the manifestation. Faith always has tangible *substance* (Heb. 11:1). Really believing something means that it will always demonstrate in my life. What you believe about yourself will explode forth in external reality. Believe who you are, and you will manifest who you really are. Know you're holy and the holy life will shine forth as a result.

Believe you're a sinner; you'll have sin.

Believe you're righteous; you'll manifest righteousness.

It is all a question of identity at the end of the day. The biggest temptation satan always threw at Jesus was to have Him question His identity. The main focus of the tempter was not the turning of stones to bread or leaping off the temple. The repeated temptation was to succumb to this nagging doubt: *If you are the Son of God. ...*

Satan wanted Jesus to doubt His very identity.

You need to know who you are. You are a pure, holy child of God. There is no effort or work involved for you to *be* who you are. A tree does not labor or strive to be a tree. In the same way, you do not labor or strive to be holy. Holiness is simply your first and primary nature. Just be yourself. In the same way, your union with Christ is an effortless state of being. It takes no more work for me than being a natural born citizen of America. Being an American is simply who I am.

The moment you decide to *do something* to be holy, you have trusted in yourself, instead of Christ, for salvation.

Fighting the Phantom

You have to believe what you are. Sin is like a third shoe. It doesn't fit you anymore, because you don't even have that leg! If you have been wrestling with sin, you have been shadowboxing a lie. Struggling completely in vain. I am not telling you to pretend the sinful nature is not there. I am saying that it *doesn't even exist.* The only power that a lie has is the degree to which you believe it. To the degree that you believe you are somehow a saint/sinner mutant, you will manifest unending struggle. To the degree you believe you are

completely whole, thanks to His work, you will effortlessly shine forth Christ.

It is mistakenly believed that the Christian life is going
to be a continual struggle, a never-ending striving battle
to do what is right. People love to misquote the Apostle
Paul and assert that he struggled with "doing what he
didn't want to do." They say, "Surely Paul still had an
old, sinful nature. He constantly wrestled to do the right
thing. He had an internal war going on within himself."

This is some of the most demonic rhetoric – the most
unbiblical hogwash – and it is a core fallacy that keeps
people doubting the gospel and failing to experience
the presence of God.

Paul was talking of the devilish fruit of his old days,
when he appealed to the *law* to save him. He was
speaking of a life under religion.

The Apostle Paul was not a schizophrenic. He was not
full of God and simultaneously full of sin at the same
time. God is not sharing a bunk bed with the devil inside of you. Light and darkness do not coexist. You do
not have a little devil on one shoulder, and an angel on
the other shoulder, fighting for the steering wheel like
an old Looney Tunes cartoon! BAM!

People who misquote Paul's struggle with sin from
Romans 7 usually forget to read the preceding chapter,
Romans 6, where he clearly states that his sinful nature died and was buried with Christ. Again, you have
to read the scriptures in context. But most people just
repeat doctrines they've heard and assume they know
the storyline, rather than studying the scriptures for
themselves.

Paul just gave you an official death certificate in Romans 6 – *you died with Christ* – and he now proceeds to address the legal ramifications of such a huge event in Romans 7. Let's take a look.

Who is the Romans 7 Man?

For starters, Paul was not even addressing Romans 7 to *you*. He was serving it up to Jews who had been running the hamster wheel of religion for decades before their conversion. In verse one, he says he is "speaking to men who know the law."

The law proves to us how hopeless we are to justify ourselves by it. That's the point of the law. It sends us running into the arms of a savior! It is a tutor pointing us to the person of Christ (Gal. 3:24). Leviticus, for instance, is not exactly pleasure reading if you don't know Jesus. But with New Covenant eyes, you see that book as a prophecy of Christ's sacrifice.

Paul now explains to these former law-abiding Jews that they "died to the law" through the broken body of Christ. They no longer belong to the law, but they now belong to *Him* (Rom. 7:4).

Then Paul continues to speak *past tense* about the days when they were still sinners under the law, trying in vain to do what was right.

For when we were controlled by the sinful nature, the sinful passions aroused by the law were at work in our bodies, so that we bore fruit for death. But now, by dying to what once bound us, we have been released from the law so that we serve in the new way of the Spirit, and not in the old way of the written code (Rom. 7:5-6, NIV).

THE MYTH OF THE FLESH

44

Paul makes it dramatically clear that a change has now taken place. A New Covenant has been made in Christ. God did not save us to send us back to the law. The law was never the goal. The law was given as an antecedent to point us to Christ. Now the law is written on our hearts – internalized by the regenerating work of the Holy Spirit – and it continually points us to Him.

A lot of people know the law – even unbelievers have a *general* sense of morality. Just because someone is a non-Christian doesn't mean they aspire to be a law-breaker. Buddhists and Muslims are not out promoting pornography and child-molestation. All men have some inherent concept of right and wrong. But everyone under the law is still eating from the Tree of Knowledge of Good and Evil – the tree of right and wrong. It's the tree of "do good" and "don't do bad." It's a legal tree, but not a life-giving tree. It is a tree that produces death. The law itself is good. But it illuminates how sinful an unbeliever is. The Bible says the law actually *increases* the drive to sin (Rom. 5:20)! And it rightly pronounces a just sentence of death toward the sinner. A good thing that produces death. The Tree of Knowledge of Good and Evil was not bad in itself, but it did produce death in the one who ate from it. Everything God created in the Garden was good. But when man ate from it to gain God-likeness (something he already had) the tree produced death.

If you think you're still a sinner, you will try to fight off evil with good. That is a return to the law. A return to self-justification. And the law just amplifies the drive to sin drive.

We no longer eat from the law. There was another tree in the Garden ... the *Tree of Life!* Jesus Christ is the Fruit of the Tree of Life. The moment you eat from Him, you live forever.

If the apostle Paul no longer had a sinful nature, why did he claim to do the things he didn't want to do?

After Paul makes it clear that a change has taken place, thanks to the cross, he begins to further elaborate on it in Romans 7. He now begins a *parabolic* discourse. Although he uses present-tense language, he begins to speak *hypothetically* to make a point. The point he is making is that – while still under the law – that law only served to provoke sin. It proved how sinful Paul really was in that unconverted state. Pay attention to my contextual notes in the following passage:

We know that the law is spiritual; but I am unspiritual (hypothetically speaking, in my unsaved state), *sold as a slave to sin. I do not understand what I do. For what I want to do I do not do, but what I hate I do. And if I do what I do not want to do, I agree that the law is good* (i.e. I am aware of the goodness of the law, but cannot perform it as a sinner). *As it is, it is no longer I myself who do it, but it is sin living in me. I know that nothing good lives in me, that is, in my sinful nature* (I am aware of this even in my unsaved state). *For I have the desire to do what is good, but I cannot carry it out* (because I am powerless to do right without Christ). *For what I do is not the good I want to do; no, the evil I do not want to do—this I keep on doing. Now if I do what I do not want to do, it is no longer I who do it, but it is sin living in me that does it* (Rom. 7:14-20, NIV, notes mine).

Prior to this passage, Paul immediately gave a long, elaborate explanation how his sinful nature died. Now he is stepping back in time, hypothetically explaining how powerless he was to do the right thing, before that sinful nature was crucified. When Paul was under the law, that law only amplified his drive to sin.

This is why at the end of Romans 7 he poses a hypothetical question for the unbeliever, "What a wretched man I am! Who will rescue me from this body of death?" And then he gives the glorious answer, "Thank God – *He has done it through Jesus Christ our Lord*" (Rom. 7:25, BECK).

It is *Jesus* who set Him free from that body of death! It is *Jesus* who set him free from the sinful nature! Whenever someone is saved, the battle against sin is decisively *over.*

Rescued From the Body of Death

Don't believe the hype about how difficult temptation will be – nor how the devil will immediately come after you to make things difficult when you get saved. You crossed over from the kingdom of darkness into light. Lift your expectations for this glorious new existence. You are now evil free. Not half good/half evil. The "body of sin" and all its corresponding curses no longer cleave to you.

Renowned Bible commentator Dr. Adam Clarke says that Paul could not possibly be speaking of himself in his present state as a believer in Romans 7, because the entire chapter relates to the *cure* of sin.

"Therefore, by *I* here he cannot mean *himself,* nor any *Christian believer;* if the contrary could be proved the argument of the apostle would go to demonstrate the insufficiency of the *Gospel,* as well as the *law.* ... It is difficult to conceive how the opinion could have crept into the church, or prevailed there, that the apostle speaks here of his *regener-*

ate state; and that what was, *in* such a state, true of himself, must be true of all others in the same state! This opinion has most pitifully and most shamefully not only lowered the standard of Christianity, but destroyed its influence and disgraced its character. It requires but little knowledge of the spirit of the Gospel, and of the scope of this epistle, to see that the apostle is here either personating a Jew, under the law and without the Gospel, or showing what his own state was when he was deeply convinced that by the deeds of the law no man could be justified; and had not as yet heard those blessed words, *Brother Saul, the Lord Jesus that appeared unto thee in the way, hath sent me that thou mightest receive thy sight, and be filled with the Holy Ghost.—Acts 9:17."* [7]

Teacher W.E. Shepard agrees, writing, "He is describing the case of one *'in the flesh'* under the law. Not that he was in the flesh at the time of that writing, for he says, as just quoted, 'For when we *were in* the flesh,' showing here past experience. Being in the flesh, he had the experience of death worked in him, and, of course, could not please God." [8]

You *must* understand who this Romans 7 man is. Paul never meant that the Romans 7 man was the normative experience for the Christian life! Paul is not a professing schizophrenic. The only Christian who is a Romans 7 man is one who has fallen back under the law to fix himself up, and thus alienating himself from grace. Don't let religion fool you.

---

[7] Adam Clarke, *Commentary on the Whole Bible* (Eight Volumes, 1810-1826. Available online at http://www.godrules.net). Excerpt from Romans 7.

[8] William Shepard, *Wrested Scriptures Made Plain or, Help for Holiness Skeptics* (Louisville: Pentecostal Herald Press, 1900).

The main question is not "when" the Romans 7 man exists (i.e. *before or after salvation?*). No, here is the main question we should ask: *who* is this Romans 7 man? Thank God he is not you!

The War is Over

If the Romans 7 man is not the born-again believer, then we must begin to sort through all the ramifications. This single revelation is like a glorious explosion that detonates a world of heresy and leaves us dumbstruck, sorting through the theological rubble.

This means that we can no longer accept the idea of an internalized war going on within the believer. There is not a tension within you between light and darkness. God is sick of schizophrenic Christianity. When Jesus said, "It is finished" – and again, when He said, "Be of good cheer, I have overcome the world" – He was not giving you a Tony Robbins motivational pep speech. He wasn't bluffing just to pump you up and pretend your problems don't exist. He meant it. The enemy has been defeated.

Most churchgoers are duped into believing that there's a constant war waging within the individual Christian between the Holy Spirit and the "lusts of the flesh." Because they have misread Romans 7, it is no wonder that they also misread Galatians 5. Here, Paul tells us:

> So I say, live by the Spirit, and you will not gratify the desires of the sinful nature. For the sinful nature desires what is **contrary** to the Spirit, and the Spirit what is **contrary** to the sinful nature. They are in **conflict** with each other, so that you do not do what you want. But if you are led by the Spirit, you are not under law (Gal. 5:16-18, NIV).

THE MYTH OF THE FLESH

49

You cannot live both by the Spirit and by the sinful nature. The two are in "conflict" with one another. Or in other words, they are *contrary* to one another. The two are not co-existing within the individual. These are two separate governing entities. You are ruled either by one or another. They are rightly in conflict, but not inside a single personality. You don't have a "Spirit day," then go have a "flesh day." They are two opposite existences.

Imagine taking two strong magnets and trying to push them together by their positive or negative ends. The magnets repel one another. They can't be present together in the same space. They are *contrary* to one another. They stand in stark opposition.

Paul is talking about two, separate domineering forces within two non-overlapping realms. For the person who tries to clean himself up by following the rule of law, he is still under the domineering influence of sin. For the person who is born again, he is now under the governing influence of God. He is in *unio mystica* with the Holy Spirit.

In the same way, people misquote James when he speaks of "your lusts that war in your members." But James is speaking not of an internalized war within an individual. He speaks of divisions and feuding within the church itself. The first part of that verse asks, "But what about the feuds and struggles that exist among you?" (Jas. 4:1, PHI).

If we continue to read the passage in Galatians 5, Paul makes it clear that you are not bipolar, possessing two dual natures. This is an external war. And it is won as far as you are concerned. For only a few verses later, he sums up the passage saying:

Those who belong to Christ Jesus have crucified the sinful nature with its passions and desires (Gal. 5:24, NIV).

Tempted by Bliss

Again, we do not say it is *impossible* for a Christian to sin. If you have a momentary lapse in judgment, then surely don't camp there! *Be who you really are.* Sin is not your identity and should never be your expectancy. Stop anticipating that your whole life is going to be a huge bout with temptation. When you are born again, you are given new, God-centered longings and desires. You lose your desire to sin. Your desire to sin is just as appealing as to eat a handful of dirt. It doesn't attract you.

Of course, you have desires for pleasure. But that's not the sinful nature. The sinful nature was the thing that caused you to fulfill your desires in something other than God. At best, you could only do a half-baked job of that. To be a true hedonist – a true pleasure seeker – you will eventually have to look to God for satisfaction.

Stop fearing the power of sin to grab you. Some Christians walk around deathly afraid that they are going to accidentally sin. That is as silly as walking around worried and afraid, expecting that you are going to accidentally eat that handful of dirt today. Even Puritan theologian John Owen, who is responsible for much of our misunderstanding of Romans 7, wrote, "To suppose that whatever God requireth of us that we have power of ourselves to do, is to make the cross and grace of Jesus Christ of none effect." [9]

[9] John Owen, *The Complete Works of John Owen, Vol. 3* (London: Johnstone and Hunter, 1850-53), 433.

Stop expecting failure. Jesus never would have in-
structed His disciples to ask that they *not* be led into
temptation, unless it was possible for Him to actually
fulfill that prayer! Yes, it is possible for the believer to
live a temptation-free existence. How would you like for
all of your temptations to be *holy* temptations? I am
tempted to dive into the pleasure of His presence today! I am tempted to be drunk on the Holy Spirit! Ha!

For some reason, we believe God will answer just
about every part of the Lord's prayer, except for the no
temptation part. We believe His Kingdom can manifest
on Earth as it is in Heaven. We believe He'll give us our
daily bread. We believe He'll forgive us our trespasses.
But for some reason, Christians think it's impossible to
live a temptation-free life. In fact, lots of folks think they
get bonus points for enduring a painstaking bout with
the tempter.

If you *do* get tempted, there is nothing wrong with you.
Just rest in your identity as a new creation. Know that
there is abundant grace for you to effortlessly resist it.
Move on, not in your own power – but in the reality that
you are no longer a sinner. The reality is that your new
desires can only be fulfilled in God. Just view temptation as an adventure – it only serves as a *contrast* to
confirm who you really are. Satan questioned Jesus, *if
He really was the Son of God*. But the first words Jesus
heard before he went in the desert from the Father
were, "This is my dearly loved Son, who brings me
great joy" (Matt. 3:17, NLT).

For one, the tempter served to confirm the opposite of
what Jesus really was. Secondly, you must understand
that Jesus was tempted *for you* in the wilderness. It
was part of His redemptive act. Something He endured
so you don't have to.

THE MYTH OF THE FLESH

The law is powerless to protect you from temptation. It will only incite more sin. This is because the law can only give you a "No." Do not eat this. Do not touch that. The Spirit of God never gives you a "No." He is the eternal "Yes!" Jesus, unlike the law, is the eternal *substitute*. He substitutes your longings for unholy pleasures and replaces them with better, higher desires for *holy* pleasures! His pleasures far outweigh the temporal mirage of sin. And yet, the pleasures of God are not somewhere in outer space, unattainable. They are real and concrete, fulfilling and immediate. They are closer than the air you breathe.

Again, your desire for pleasure is not sinful. You are *created for it*. You were created to find it *in God* who is the delicious fountainhead of rivers of pleasure forevermore (Ps. 36:8). He even gives you natural pleasures – marital love, money, health – as long as they are filtered through the Word and not idolized.

Christ as You

There is only one way that a believer can slip into a Romans 7 scenario of "wrestling" to do the right thing. He cannot cease to trust in the finished work of the cross, hence rest in the risen Christ as his permanent Indweller.

As a new believer, we have a new master. This thrills us with excitement. One of the first things we want to do is please Him! This seems innocent enough, but it is where Romans 7 can kick in. God didn't save you so that you can do good. He saved you so you could be dead and He could work through you. He doesn't want you trying to please Him. He is only pleased with Christ. We don't labor to earn something from God, or even to impress Him. We labor for the simple sake of the joy and pleasure of God *within* the tasks at hand. We pursue labor for the inherent fun in the call itself.

I no longer even have an independent self that is capable of pleasing God. It is no longer *I* but Christ. As new believers, we run off half-cocked trying to perform a dog and pony show. We still conceive of a separate independent existence from Him, wherein we must please Him. All we have ever known was separation in the fallen world. We don't have a concept of *union*. There is no separate, individual *you*. Christ has *replaced* you.

It must be Him who wills and works to do His good pleasure in us. As a new creation, we have been crucified and replaced.

Defining the Flesh

Allow me a moment to switch gears. After all, this chapter is titled the "Myth of the Flesh," and so I'd better get on with explaining myself a bit along those lines. Often people get confused because of messy, cliché Christian language. There is a lot of talk about "overcoming the flesh." If you see any minister peddling a teaching on their book table explaining "How to overcome the flesh," you can know for certain that this is a man who doesn't know the gospel. Not saying he isn't *saved* – just probably has no clue what he's saved from!

Lots of folks don't really have a clear definition for the "flesh." And that's because the word is used in two different ways in the New Testament.

Used in one sense, *flesh* is simply your physical body. There is absolutely *nothing* wrong with your body. Your body is just a meat sack – sinews, muscles, and ligaments. It is not evil. In fact, it is *amoral*. It is simply a physical, material vehicle that is driven by the one who owns it.

Jesus also had a fleshly body. In fact, He still has that human body in a glorified, resurrected form! You will one day touch Him with His skin on. Never let someone fool you into believing He is now just a shiny cloud in outer space. The same body that walked in Nazareth is raised immortal.

Just because something is in the physical, material world does not make it evil. That is the extreme heresy of gnosticism. Gnostics believed that any material-world thing is evil, and that all "spiritual" or "unseen" things are good. That is why gnostics denied that Jesus came in the flesh. In their mind, he could not have had a body, because such physical objects are evil.

The Apostle John vehemently corrects this very gnostic lie. He says that anyone who denies Jesus came in the flesh is of the *antichrist* (2 John 1:7). It is a serious perversion even to suggest that your physical body is wicked. Your body is a temple of the Holy Spirit, bought at a high price (1 Cor. 6:19-20).

God is not shacked up with the devil inside His temple!

God is light; in Him there is no darkness at all (1 John 1:5, NIV).

The Lord is not joined together with darkness. Light and darkness cannot co-exist. For Christ to become sin meant that sin must necessarily be abolished on the cross. God made Christ who *knew no sin to be sin on our behalf, so that we might become the righteousness of God in Him* (1 Cor. 5:21, NASB). For Christ to "be-

55

come darkness" meant it was annulled by light. You can't cram darkness into a lit room without it dissolving.

"Where, except in uncreated light, can the darkness be drowned?" asked C.S. Lewis.[10] Flipping on the switch means that darkness flees the room. Light and darkness have no fellowship. Christ has no fellowship with a false sinful identity, *for the sinful nature is always hostile to God* (Rom. 8:7, NLT). When Christ came into your life, how long did the process take for the darkness to flee? Did it take 40 years of inner healing classes? No. It happened instantaneously. The light bulb cleared the room. A transformation took place where you were changed from a sinner into a saint. Stop fighting yourself and stop looking down on your physical body. Our bodies are now *instruments of righteousness* to be used for God's Glory (Rom. 6:13).

So if our physical bodies are not evil, then why does the *flesh* get a bad rap? Well, there is a second usage of the word *flesh*. Always used in a negative sense, it indicates the "lusts of the flesh." Its New Testament use simply refers to the old *naughty self*. The "bad flesh" is not your body. It's defined as the *carnal nature with its appetites and its lusts*. The term is synonymous with the *sinful nature*, or the *old man*. It is the old, self-seeking existence that died with Christ – and you first realized it at conversion. You don't have it anymore.

It is a myth that Christians must overcome their flesh.

---

[10] C.S. Lewis, *Letters to Malcolm Chiefly on Prayer* (San Diego and New York: Harcourt, Inc., 1973).

Part 2 ... **SANCTIFICATION IS NOT A PROCESS**

Okay, *what's the deal* you're asking? What's with all the deconstructionist chapter titles? First you take away my *flesh* (my sinful nature), now you want to take away my sanctification process as well? How dare you!

All I can say is, buckle up friend. This goes a lot deeper than you realize. The church has a lot of cardboard wadding shoved into its foundation and termites have eaten right through the basement walls. Don't blame me, I'm just telling you this thing isn't built to code.

The most scholarly minds all agree that a mystical death with Christ purchased union with Him. But then a theological dishonesty creeps in. We are next taught that – although the old man is dead – we still have a *daily process* of putting that old self to death. *I die daily* is a common motto!

They call it a *paradox*. Two opposites that are held in tension. They say your fleshly nature is dead, yet it is still in need of crucifixion. *Paradox indeed!* I call this a lack of revelation at best. Lazy exegesis at worst. The scriptures never contradict themselves. The word "paradox" sounds fun, but there are far fewer of them in scripture than you would imagine. *Lobotomy* is a fun word as well, but I don't want one. People think, "We haven't figured it out, so it must be an unsolvable puzzle! A paradox!" There are no unsolvable puzzles. Every mystery has been plainly published on the tree.

The word people use for this supposed process of killing the old self is "sanctification." It is widely believed that sanctification is a lifelong, extended journey of *becoming holy*. A process of removing sin – progressively having one's soul purged over an entire lifetime.

The Greek verb "to sanctify" does not mean to "purge and purify over a period of time." The word *hagiazo* simply means to "set apart" or to "make separate for God."[11] The moment you were saved, you were set apart for God. Sanctification is not a process. It is a *Person*. The Bible tells me so!

*And because of Him you are in **Christ Jesus, who became** to us wisdom from God, righteousness and **sanctification** and redemption* (1 Cor. 1:30, ESV).

He is your sanctification. Any system that tries to draw your attention away from the person of Christ and onto your own efforts is antichrist in nature. Your union with God is not an incomplete relationship that comes progressively. Time is not the magic formula that makes you holy. Jesus' sacrifice made you holy. Christ's work was enough to purify you, spirit, soul and body.

Often, when intellectuals cannot explain something adequately, they use the element of "time" as a magic ingredient to cover up their lack of understanding. For instance, how can brilliant scientists really believe a ridiculous fallacy such as evolution? How did humans defeat the exponentially impossible odds to evolve from inanimate mud? Simple. Add a magic ingredient called "billions and billions of years!" Anybody will believe it!

The same is true to explain the lack of fruit in the unconverted soul. Why is this supposed Christian still living in sin? "Oh, because it takes *years and years* to sanctify you! Then you will have a sin-free life!"

---

[11] James Strong, *Exhaustive Concordance of the Bible* (Nashville: Abingdon, 1890), Entry 37.

Think of how the word "sanctification" is used in other places in the New Testament, none of which ever require a time element or involve a long grueling process. Here are a few examples:

With food:
For everything created by God is good, and nothing is to be rejected if it is received with gratitude; it is sanctified (hagiazo) by means of the word of God and prayer (1 Tim. 4:4-5, NASB).

All it takes is one blessing to sanctify your hamburger! No inner healing program necessary. Your food is going to get cold if you spend too much time saying the blessing.

With the Father's name:
He said to them, "When you pray, say: "Father, hallowed (hagiazo) be your name, your Kingdom come. ..." (Luke 11:2, NIV).

Not going to see many translators write, "Father let your name be sanctified" because it doesn't jive with the process theology they have attached to the word. Does the Father's name need to be purged and purified? Does the Father need a deep inner healing or deliverance class? No. We recognize that the Father's name is "set apart."

With the Son:
Do you say of Him, whom the Father sanctified (hagiazo) and sent into the world, "You are blaspheming," because I said, "I am the Son of God?" (John 10:36, NASB)

Here, we read that Jesus was sanctified by the Father. Does that mean it took His whole life to get cleaned up from his sordid past? Did Jesus go through a 12-step

59

program or years of therapy? No. He was simply "set apart" just like you.

Evangelism of the Heart

One popular phrase coined by progressive sanctification proponents is this: *The entire heart needs to be evangelized.* By this, they mean that the entire inner man needs to be saved bit by bit. This phrase, *evangelizing the heart*, sounds catchy and romantic. In fact, I agree that the heart needs to be evangelized. But it happens in one fell swoop.

The Lord tells us in the book of Ezekiel that, "I will give you a new heart and put a new spirit in you; I will remove from you your heart of stone and give you a heart of flesh" (Ezek. 36:26, NIV). God removed the old, hardened heart that was cold and unloving. He gave you in its place a new, tender, touchable heart.

Now, wouldn't God be a cruel masochist if your entire life were a long, bloody open-heart surgery, where He removed your heart bit by bit? This heart transplant was a one-time transaction. The old is gone; the new has come.

Did you know that it was *His own* heart that He gave you? I am not talking about an amalgamated, pantheistic absorption of your personality. Yes, you do have a unique personality, but it is so melded and united to His that Paul could rightly say the following:

I consider myself as having died and now I'm enjoying a new existence which is simply Jesus using my body (Gal. 2:20, DIS).

In a very real sense, Christ has replaced you!

Christians don't usually have a problem believing that Jesus lives inside of them. The thing that is really hard to swallow is that the devil *doesn't* live in you anymore!

It is true that our heart is growing to trust and believe more and more. But it is still a *new heart* that is growing in faith. Not the old one.

You Have Fullness

Paul told the Colossians that in Jesus Christ, the whole fullness of the Godhead lives in bodily form (Col. 2:9). That means Holy Spirit was in Jesus; the Father was in Jesus; and of course, there was Jesus Himself. The entire triune God. Paul continues to write:

> *And, by your union with Him, you also are filled with it* (Col. 2:10, TCNT).

What are you filled with? Just Holy Spirit alone? No. Your mystical union with Christ fills you with the entire Godhead. That means Jesus is in you. It also means the Father of Lights lives within you – the One who breathed the very stars into existence. He's right here, fully inside of you!

You don't just have a little portion of God. Not just one percent of Him. Not just a little Bobby or Suzy sized version. You have the *fullness* of the Godhead in there. All thanks to your union with Christ. If you started to actually believe how much heat you're packing inside of you, you could change the world in a single day.

So many people are paranoid of the devil. They attribute so much to him, as if he were God's equal and opposite adversary. As if God and the devil were sitting up in Heaven playing chess, wondering who will win. As an itinerate minister, I travel all over the world. It is amazing how often I find paranoid Christians. How often am I in the boonies of some random little town – and someone says, "Yes, this place is where satan has his headquarters. The throne of satan is in our little town of Swampwater, West Virginia. It's so hard for us here. We have the highest drug and prostitution rate per capita in the entire world. It's really hard for us here. Lots and lots of warfare. We need to blow our shofars harder and wave our worship banners more often fend off all the attacks!"

And I'm thinking, "But you only have four people in your town. Don't you think satan would get bored living here?"

I wish this were an exaggeration, but so many people think this way! They are always talking about principalities of darkness and warfare and witches and dragons and conspiracy theories. It makes my head spin at the superstition and utter lack of revelation of the gospel. I don't know much about warfare, but I know a lot about *joyfare*. I don't know much about your principalities, but I know a lot about mine. Colossians 2:10 continues to tell us He is:

The head of all principality and power (KJV).

The fountain head from which all dominion and power proceed (KNOX).

The authority over all authorities, and the supreme power over all powers (PHI).

He is the highest ruler over every other power (TAY).

This is the Godhead who lives right inside of you! You have an inexhaustible and eternal source of power, dominion and exhilarating joy living inside of you. All of God lives within you thanks to your union with Christ. The devil is not a bit scared of your shofars and worship banners, but the blood of Christ did a tremendous job of defeating him.

It is amazing how often I hear people talk about "pressing in" for more of God's fullness. They have all sorts of little formulas and methods that they think will give them more of God. Whether it's an ascetic fasting and prayer routine, or something more bizarre. They think they have to *overcome their flesh* or beat up the devil to get more of God. But the Bible clearly states that you already have fullness because of your union with Christ! You are already hooked up to the fullness valve.

If you think it is up to you to take hold of God's fullness, how far along are you? Two percent? Twelve percent? Anybody ever get hold of ninety-eight percent of God?

Sounds ridiculous, eh? You have all of Him or nothing.

Circumcision of the Heart

In this same passage of Colossians 2, Paul jumps immediately from discussing your union with the fullness of the Godhead right into a very strange topic ... *circumcision.*

Ouch! Sounds painful I know ... but relax. He says it is a circumcision made without a bodily operation – not a physical circumcision done by man's handiwork. This is a mystical act. It is a circumcision of the heart.

You may not be a specialist physician, but I hope you understand what circumcision entails. It means that something is *cut off!* I will spare you the graphic, anatomical explanations here, but you get the picture.

Something has been completely cut away. Chopped off once and for all. And guess what that something is?

> In the circumcision of Christ you were **set free from your sinful nature** (Col. 2:11, NOR).

Again, Paul reiterates this same reality. _The gospel cuts away the sinful nature._ This death of the old man is the foundational mysticism of St. Paul. In the next verse, he relates circumcision to the same spiritual death you died in baptism:

> You, by baptism, have been **united with His burial, united, too, with His resurrection**, through your faith ... (Col. 2:12, KNOX).

Just as we received a singular heart transplant, so likewise did we receive a singular circumcision of the heart. The sinful nature was circumcised off. That thing is not still hanging on.

Aren't you glad that circumcision is not a _daily process?_ It would give the term "I die daily" a whole new meaning! No. Circumcision is a one-time occurrence that Christ performed mystically on the cross. Joshua (lit. Yeshua, a type of Christ) circumcised the entire army of Israel by his own hand when they first entered the Promised Land. In the same way, Christ circumcised of the entire corporate entity of sinfulness, bringing us into a land of new existence. You now have unadulterated access into the Most Holy Place. You are now in permanent residence in the land of milk and honey.

Oh, how we should revel in the joys of the cross! It is not a somber place where we must go to suffer and die. It is the place where the feast lay before us. The place where we have _already_ mystically died with Him!

It is your get out of jail free card. You did not even feel the pain of it.

You are an Isaac company. Isaac means laughter. Isaac means "Ha! Ha! Ha!" We are a people of promise, a people of Ha! Ha! Ha! Martin Luther once said that the gospel is nothing less than laughter and joy. You are not the slavish people of Ishmael. Ishmael was fully grown when he was circumcised. He had to feel the pain, because he represented the old, do-it-yourself covenant on Sinai. But little baby Isaac was different! He was only eight days old when he was circumcised. Isaac doesn't even remember what happened to him. He has no memory of the pain. Your death found its substitution in Christ – He took the bullet for you!

I Die Daily

Just as it would be foolish to think we have a daily heart transplant or a daily circumcision ... in the same way, it is foolish to think death to self is a daily process. Death is a finite event. Not a continuous prolonging.

Have you heard the term "I die daily?" I know you have. It's a very common Christian cliché. People even know to attribute the phrase to the Apostle Paul. I have done an informal case study in dozens of revival meetings. From a regular show of hands, about 99 percent of people know the term "I die daily." But only about five percent remember reading the scripture in context.

When you read the Bible, you realize that Paul was absolutely *not* talking about a daily crucifixion of his old sinful self. The Apostle Paul was talking about facing the dangers of *persecution* on a constant basis!

"How often have we heard those who believe in a gradual process of sanctification quote this text to prove their argument!" writes author W.E. Shepard. "Nowhere do we find that the Scriptures teach a daily dying in order to get sanctified. Neither do they teach, that after one is sanctified, there is any further dying out to carnality. And especially does the text, 'I die daily,' have no reference to either thought. Then, what does Paul mean by the expression? ... Paul is stating that his life is in jeopardy every day and every hour."[12]

St. Paul was not talking about an introverted, masochistic killing of his own inward self. Paul's former self was not merely crippled, paralyzed or maimed. His old nature was not merely left dormant, suppressed or pacified. Nor was the sinful self left half-dead or narcoticized. He was *killed*. Dead to sin and alive to God. It was this very revelation that stirred trouble for him! He was persecuted for the blissful message of the gospel.

Are they servants of Christ? I am a better one—I am talking like a madman—with far greater labors, far more imprisonments, with countless beatings, and often near death. Five times I received at the hands of the Jews the forty lashes less one. Three times I was beaten with rods. Once I was stoned. Three times I was shipwrecked; a night and a day I was adrift at sea; on frequent journeys, in danger from rivers, danger from robbers, danger from my own people, danger from Gentiles, danger in the city, danger in the wilderness, danger at sea, danger from false brothers; in toil and hardship, through many a sleepless night, in hunger and thirst, often without food, in cold and exposure. And, apart from other things, there is the daily

<hr>

[12] William Shepard, *Wrested Scriptures Made Plain or, Help for Holiness Skeptics.*

pressure on me of my anxiety for all the churches (2 Cor. 11:23-28, ESV).

Reading this, you realize why Paul said this: *I myself run the risk of dying every single day* (1 Cor. 15:31, WMS). Paul faced the firing squad everyday – he was a code red security risk. He even caught heat from the top notch "super-apostles" – even men sent from James, the brother of Jesus! Imagine the top-notch prophets of the charismatic circuit coming down on you, because they don't fully understand the message of grace you are preaching. On top of that, Paul had the daily pressure of all the churches – the stress of running the company as a CEO. And that was just on top of the shipwrecks, beatings, etc. At least the Jews stopped beating him at 39 lashes (they thought they were being merciful by not giving the full 40 prescribed by the law). But the Gentiles would beat him all day long. If the Jews had a hypocritical conscience, the Gentiles had none at all.

When reading "I die daily" in context, we must include the preceding verse. There, you see that he didn't just die everyday. He said it happened every *hour*.

Besides, why do we live dangerously every moment? (1 Cor. 15:30, BER)

Why also do we apostles take such risks every hour? (1 Cor. 15:30, WEY)

And I too, why do I put my life to hazard every hour? (1 Cor. 15:30, CON).

And why do you think I keep risking my neck in this dangerous work? I look death in the face practically every day I live. Do you think I'd do this if I wasn't convinced of your resurrection and mine as guaran-

67

teed by the resurrected Messiah Jesus? Do you think I was just trying to act heroic when I fought the wild beasts at Ephesus, hoping it wouldn't be the end of me? Not on your life! It's resurrection, resurrection, always resurrection, that undergirds what I do and say, the way I live. If there's no resurrection, "We eat, we drink, the next day we die," and that's all there is to it. But don't fool yourselves. Don't let yourselves be poisoned by this anti-resurrection loose talk. "Bad company ruins good manners" (1 Cor. 15:30-33, MSG).

Why was Paul so hazard prone? First of all, the scandalous message of grace attracts major persecution. When Paul stopped preaching the do-it-yourself law of physical circumcision and started preaching the free gift of the cross of Christ, it made him very controversial.

As for the rumor that I continue to preach the ways of circumcision (as I did in those pre-Damascus Road days), that is absurd. Why would I still be persecuted, then? If I were preaching that old message, no one would be offended if I mentioned the Cross now and then—it would be so watered-down it wouldn't matter one way or the other. Why don't these agitators, obsessive as they are about circumcision, go all the way and castrate themselves! (Gal. 5:11-12, MSG)

Don't think Paul was just some unusually tough character to be able to handle all this kind of flack. He didn't just have the gung ho of a Marine Corp sergeant. Paul was tapping into a *joy unspeakable* that fueled him. The Holy Spirit is like a glorious anesthesia that enables you to endure any kind of external trial. Otherwise, why didn't the apostles always cry and suck their thumbs when being afflicted, rather than jumping, leaping and shouting for joy? Paul was running on a million volts of bliss, which drove him into crazy situations.

*Yours is the bliss, when men shall heap their insults on you, and persecute you, and tell every wicked kind of lie about you for my sake. When that happens, **rejoice and exult in it**, for you will receive a rich reward in Heaven ... (Matt. 5:11-12, BNT).*

Is this just a future joy that you will experience in Heaven after suffering down here? No. Heaven is right here, right now for the born-again believer.

*O the bliss of those who are persecuted for their loyalty to God's way of life, for the blessings of the Kingdom of Heaven are theirs **here and now** (Matt. 5:10, BNT).*

This is bliss in the midst of the storm. You're never disconnected from God.

Taking up Your Cross

Stop looking at sufferings and persecutions from an outward, external perspective. Although Stephen was being stoned in the body, yet he was experiencing a rapturous, out-of-body experience seeing Jesus sitting at the right hand of the Father (Acts 7). Paul clearly remembered the death of this first martyr. He stood there that day, batting for the other team. Paul was the jacket caddie while the fat cat Pharisees shot bogies.

You have to understand that Paul was not depressed while going through these persecutions. Persecution does not equal depression. In fact, it ignites a wellspring of supernatural bliss and Glory within you. These brief troubles don't hold a candle to the immeasurable weight of Glory they produce in us (2 Cor. 4:17).

Because you are in union with Christ, He does not leave you to suffer for Him alone. The Lord promises innumerable blessings to us through the atonement. Forgiveness. Healing. Prosperity. Supernatural power. Reconciliation. Adoption. Joy. The blessings are endless. But ... *He also guarantees persecution to His followers!* Yet, He makes this an easy pill to swallow with His deep consolations, so there's no room for self-pity. *The blessings always outweigh it all, both now and later. On top of that, remember that *it is not Jesus* who is persecuting you! He loves you! So don't misjudge Him.!

He also doesn't want you to be an ignorant dolt and go out looking for trouble and self-harm. He actually tells us to *avoid* persecution, unless love or righteousness requires it at the moment. Don't take a spirit of suicide onboard. Suicide and religion are the same thing.

Hopefully, this should now clarify another often misunderstood verse, *"If anyone wishes to come after Me, he must deny himself, and take up his cross daily and follow Me"* (Luke 14:27, NASB). Simply put, Jesus is saying *lose sight of yourself.* On one hand, we should be ready for persecution and troubles to come if we are going to follow Him. But even in that, His yoke is easy and light. The Lord doesn't say that tribulations won't come. But He does promise to bring you through them with joy unspeakable and full of Glory! Don't be self-focused, but be God-focused. It's really *Him* suffering through you.

In no way is Jesus saying you have to die for your own sinfulness by carrying your own cross. Nor is He saying that you still have a sinful nature to continually destroy.

He Took Your Cross

At the end of the day, you really don't even get to carry your own cross. This is such an idol in the church! Religious people love to boast about the "cross they are carrying."

When Jesus talks about denying yourself and taking up your cross, this is really a passage about ceasing from your own self-efforts and self-driven attempts at spiritual advancement. Let *self* be smudged totally out of the equation.

"In the eternal sense this verse means that we are to follow after Christ's sacrifice, not mimic it, but trust in it alone for our salvation and sustainment," writes our friend Ben Dunn in *The Happy Gospel*. "The sense here in this scripture is not self-sacrifice in the way that most would see it. It actually is a call to deny any heavenly advancement through self-achievement."[13]

Let me ask you a question. If you get to carry your own cross, then whose cross did Jesus die upon?

Did He deserve His cross? I'm sorry ... I may have missed something here. ... What *sin* did Jesus commit to deserve His cross? What *crime* was done to merit such punishment? Oh ... wait a minute friend. He didn't commit a crime ... *you did!* Jesus was carrying *your punishment.* Any system of religious belief that puts the emphasis on what you need to do for the Lord, rather than what He has done for you, detracts from the Glory of God and spits on the work of the gospel.

---

[13] Benjamin Dunn, *The Happy Gospel* (Santa Cruz, CA: Joy Revolution, 2010), 102-103.

God actually *wants* to boast in single-handedly saving the world.

Christianity was originally called *good news*. It used to be a happy message that people wanted to be a part of. The original version of the gospel seemed too good to be true. That's why it spread like wildfire. Heaven as a free gift. Your sinfulness abolished. Effortless union with God. Amazing benefits! Easy, instant soul purge.

Let me tell you, if the gospel you've heard is not too good to be true, it probably isn't. The frequency of the gospel always inspires, always brings life and hope. The flavor and sound of the true gospel never puts rule and regulation and heavy trips on you. Never makes you feel you have to live up to any systematic expectations for acceptance. It always encourages, always hopes, always trusts, and always loves.

Some would accuse us of preaching a candy-coated gospel. That's not entirely true. This gospel is not just candy-coated. It also has bubble gum in the middle.

Self-Distrust

The gospel is truly a one-step program. Verses of scripture that are misquoted or taken out of context so as to indicate that sanctification is an "ongoing process" often confuse people.

One of these common misinterpretations leads people to believe we must "work out our salvation" with *fear and trembling*. Sounds like a big, scary responsibility!

Opening your Bible and plopping your finger down on a random verse to hear the word of the Lord is no better than using a ouija board. But that's how people throw around these verses, having no grid for their contextual meaning. This verse is a classic example.

Here is the scenario in context. When Paul was writing to the Philippians, he was in prison. He knew that the odds were stacked against him to ever return to Philippi again. It is for this reason that he told the Philippians they would need to sort out the goodies of salvation on their own. Paul would no longer be around to warn them of the Judaizing legalists. They would need to grow up and not just drink from Paul's revelation any longer. Arthur S. Way translates this verse brilliantly:

*Since I am far away ... work out, with fear and **self-distrust**, ay, with **trembling self-distrust**, your own salvation. **You have not to do it in your un-aided strength**: it is **God** who is all the while sup-plying the impulse, giving you the power to resolve, the strength to perform, the execution of His good-pleasure* (Phil. 2:12-13, WAY).

Paul is actually saying here that we should not rely on our *own efforts* for this salvation! He is saying don't trust yourself to handle this honey pot. Distrust yourself! It is God who does it all, and it is God who you should rely upon. Is it possible that this verse actually means the *very opposite* of what we've been taught? It is not about your own sweaty work out. It is about not trusting yourself to work it out at all. It is a fearful thing to trust your own efforts for any aspect of salvation.

Freedom to Sin or From Sin?

In saying that the old nature is dead, we are not at all advocating sin. Some would foolishly believe, "Since I am no longer a sinner, now it's perfectly OK for me to sin!" This is the same ridiculous argument that Paul had to deal with in his day. It was also a core belief in the Roman version of gnosticism. For this reason, he predicated the entire passage of Romans 6 by saying:

> *Now what is our response to be? Shall we sin to our heart's content and see how far we can exploit the grace of God? What a ghastly thought! We, who have died to sin – how could we live in sin a moment longer?* (Rom. 6:1-2, PHI)

Clarence Jordan's *Cotton Patch Version of Paul's Epistles* is a bit more candid, showing just how blunt the Apostle's language is on this matter:

> *So what are we advocating? "Let's wallow in sin, so more grace may pour forth"? Hell, no!* (Rom. 6:1, CPG)

This is not freedom *to* sin; it is freedom *from* sin. Don't get into a filthy perversion of the doctrine of grace by thinking you can now go sin to your heart's content. That's stupid. Why would you sin if you are no longer a sinner? Some would pervert the intent of Paul's statement that "all things are permissible," and use it as a license to be naughty.

Because we preach on freedom from the sinful nature, we have seen some people pervert this truth, just as they did with Paul's teachings. Never be dissuaded from the truth, just because a few bandits try to push it to a heretical extreme. Samuel Taylor Coleridge once said, "Every reform, however necessary, will by weak minds be carried to an excess which will itself need reforming." Likewise, Theodore Roosevelt quipped, "Every reform movement has a lunatic fringe."

Not Becoming Holy

Holiness is both demanded and empowered. Jesus said *be perfect*. Prophetic minister Graham Cooke says this is not merely a command. Jesus speaks it into you as a benediction – just as He said *let there be light*. His word forms it within you: *be ye perfect*.

Holiness is demand and empowered, but it is also *qualified*. He clearly defines the degree and type of holiness He requires.

> *Be perfect* **as your father in Heaven is perfect** (Matt. 5:48, LNT).

How holy are you to be? As Holy as *the Father*. That's the definition and degree of this requirement. "In other words," writes Christian perfection advocate Asa Mahan, "we are here required to be as perfect, as holy, as free from all sin, in our sphere as creatures, as God is in His as our Creator and our Sovereign."[14]

Now that is a high order! If this is something that comes progressively – or something you can accomplish – please tell me how far along the holiness scale are you? Are you forty percent pure? Eighty percent pure? How about ninety-eight percent pure?

Did you know that there is no such thing as ninety-eight percent pure? Imagine a nice, cold crisp glass of sparkling water. Someone cheerfully hands it to you and says, "Enjoy this! It is ninety-eight percent pure. ... Only two percent poop particles."

---

[14] Asa Mahan, *Scripture Doctrine of Christian Perfection* (Boston: D.S. King, 1840), 7.

I don't think you want to drink that glass. There is no such thing as *partially* holy. You are either holy or you are not. There is no in-between. *Almost pure* is an imaginary concept. Would you like for your spouse to sleep with you 364 days a year, and only spend one night a year in a stranger's bed? By my calculations, that is 99.73 percent faithful. And it is not faithful at all.

You are not *becoming* holy. That is an incongruous concept. If a process were involved, then by nature it would be a process that never ends. At no point in time would you ever arrive. You are adding an unnecessary and obfuscating element to the cross – you are requiring the element of *time*.

Granted, there are numerous verses that speak of those who are "becoming holy" or "becoming sancti-fied." But this generally applies to people *corporately* becoming holy by getting saved, or else you are just looking at a bad translation of the verse in question. I will give you one example:

*For by one offering He **has perfected** forever those who are **being sanctified** (Heb. 10:14).*

As you see here, the perfection has happened *past tense*, on the cross, because he "has perfected" them. But to the naïve eye, it seems that there's still an ongoing process of sanctification in this verse. Those "being sanctified" means those coming to the saving knowledge of Jesus Christ. Simple. The same could be said that, "All of my friends are *becoming* married." This does not mean that each couple spends decades tying the knot in a tuxedo and a bridal gown. It happens in a single ceremony. Check out the *God's Word Translation*, which says, "*With one sacrifice He accomplished the work of setting them apart for God forever.*"

We do not have time to discuss every bad translation here, nor do we want to waste time with endless apologetics. But I challenge you to research any verse that seems to pull away from Christ's completed work on the cross. I guarantee it is merely a mistranslation or interpretation problem.

Will Death Save You?

Even progressive-work folks see the vanity of eternally striving with sin. Even they know the battle cannot rage on forever. Besides the element of *time*, there is one more ingredient they add to the witch's cauldron: *death*.

One day, when I die and go to Heaven, I will be holy.

OK. So you are counting on death to save you! You have just crowned death to be your savior, instead of Jesus Christ. Death, which is the wages of sin, is somehow supposed to clean you up from sin? Dr. Adam Clarke contends that this is a greater heresy than the Catholic belief in purgatory.

Wow! never thought of it like that

> *Protestants ... how positively do they hold out death as the complete deliverer from all corruption, and the final destroyer of sin, as if it were revealed in every page of the Bible! There is not one passage in the sacred volume that says any such thing. Were this true, then death, far from being the last enemy, would be the last and best friend, and the greatest of all deliverers: for if the last remains of all the indwelling sin of all believers is to be destroyed by death, (and a fearful mass this will make) then death, that removes it, must be the highest benefactor of mankind.*[15]

---

[15] Adam Clarke, "Entire Sanctification" (Available online at http://www.ccel.org/ccel/clarke/entire_sanct.titlepage.html).

SANCTIFICATION IS NOT A PROCESS

It is the blood of Jesus alone that cleanses from all un-righteousness.

In the same way, we mistakenly believe that we *go to Heaven when we die*. This is not true. You entered Heaven when Jesus died. Your death is not the door-way to Heaven. His death was the doorway to Heaven. It was your co-crucifixion with Him that has now seated you in heavenly places (Eph. 2:6).

Do I sound like a broken record yet? Does it seem I am being a stickler on my insistence that the old man is dead? I need to be loud because ninety percent of the church doesn't know it. This boast in Christ's cross – and not our own self-mortifications – was the sole rea-son for Paul's message. If I am a broken record, then you will hate Paul's letters. He resolved to *know noth-ing else* but Christ and Him crucified (1 Cor. 2:2). Be-ware of the counterfeit gospel.

Lost in Translations

We regularly encourage people to get *multiple transla-tions* of the scriptures, to truly understand the heart of the message. Although it is convenient to have just one Bible with all your notes and highlights, it can be dan-gerous to drink from just one translation. Whether you realize it or not, you may be eating one person's theol-ogy.

Progressive sanctification is such a religious strong-hold; translators who just assume we are supposed to help God clean ourselves up wrongly insert it into doz-ens of verses. It keeps a life of happy holiness distant from you, unattainable in outer space. Keeps you from daily enjoying your complete and total gift of divine un-ion. Branch out and read as many different versions as you can. When the King James folks were working on the 1611 translation, they quoted Augustine as proof "that variety of translations is profitable for the finding out of the sense of the Scriptures."[16] So if you are a "King James only" kind of person, you must obviously love a variety of translations!

People pull bits and snippets of scripture and wrongly apply them. Frankly, most people don't even know what the *gospel* is! The gospel is not Matthew, Mark, Luke and John. These are primarily historical documents that also include the teachings of Christ. Did you know that the red letters of Christ are also not the gospel? Wow! Christ's earthly ministry was a transition between the Old and New Covenants. He was fulfilling the law and mostly showing folks how futile it was to be justified by law. The New Covenant starts at the cross.

Jesus the Law Preacher

Jesus was not a grace preacher. Not only did He preach the law – He preached the law on steroids! Moses told people not to commit adultery, but Jesus said just wink at the dirty magazine in the grocery store aisle and you've already done it in your heart.

> Don't misunderstand why I have come. I did not come to abolish the law of Moses or the writings of the prophets. No, I came to accomplish their purpose (Matt. 5:17, NLT).

The point of the parables was not for you to try to do them. The point of the parables was to utterly *frustrate* you so you would cry out for a Saviour. Jesus essentially said things like, "Gonna clean *yourselves* from sin? OK, chop off your hands and pluck your eyeballs

---

[16] *The Holy Bible King James Version: 1611 Edition*, translators' introduction (S. Aug. 2. de doctr. Christian. cap. 14.).

out. The only way to save yourself from hell is to dis-member yourself."

Do you think He really expects you to mutilate your-self? The Sermon on the Mount, for instance, should make you want to give up your own hand of cards and look to His cross for salvation.

The *gospel* is not Matthew, Mark, Luke and John. The gospel is the good news of Christ's sacrifice for the re-moval of sinfulness. It is most clearly articulated through the epistles of Paul, who wrote two-thirds of the New Covenant. Just because Paul's letters are not in red ink does not make them less anointed. *They are still the words of Jesus!* Even James does not pack the full revelation of the gospel that Paul carried. James is rock solid Bible truth. But it's more of a transition book, as it is geared primarily toward Jews in Jerusalem.

Does this sound too Pauline for you? Still want to mix your grace with law? Law and grace don't mix. Put them together and you get law. Episcopal priest and author Robert Capon writes:

> ... the New Testament has a perfectly good answer to the charge that Christianity as we now have it is radically Pauline. And the answer is that God hired Paul (then called Saul) on the road to Damascus for the precise purpose of making Christianity Pauline – that is, of rescuing it from the overly "re-ligious" orientation of the exclusively Jewish-Christian Jerusalem church. The main item in Paul's job description was precisely that he knock religion in the head.[17]

---

[17] Robert Capon, *Health, Money & Love and Why We Don't Enjoy Them* (Grand Rapids: William B. Eerdmans Publishers, 1990), 33.

SANCTIFICATION IS NOT A PROCESS

Moral Code 'Christianity'

Most of the church is still eating a leftover form of Judaism. Of course, we know that we are not saved by abstaining from pork or shaving our beards a certain way. But what we have done is replaced that old legal system of justification with a new *moral code*. We think that by applying St. Paul's moral principles to our lives that somehow we become holy. For instance, if I honor my wife, don't exasperate my children and stop being selfish, then I *become* holy. This line of thinking would have Paul rolling over in his grave.

In every one of Paul's letters, he gives you your *death certificate*. He tells you that you are now in mystical union and that your old sinful self is dead. Then he explains how a dead person should act! A new creation does not sleep with the temple prostitutes, for instance. A new creation should live *this way* and *that way*. Paul wasn't giving formulas for *becoming* holy. Rather, because we now believe we are *already holy* he says, "Let me show you what that's supposed to look like." Paul was speaking to Gentiles who needed a clear definition of holiness, because they came right out of paganism.

Paul's moral codes are not a new system of law. They simply define what the new you should look like. When he talks about "walking in the Spirit," putting off old practices, etc., he is simply telling you to *be who you already are*.

> *... for you have finished with the old man and all he did and have begun life as the new man, who is out to learn what he ought to be, according to the plan of God* (Col. 3:10, PHI).

81

Capon writes, "We slip into the stupor of imagining there are things we have to do – some additive of religious works we have to put into the gasoline of grace – if the gift of God is to get its work done in us. And the sad thing about it is that we'll scour the New Testament ... for every moral 'requirement' and religious 'condition' we can find in order to slap a behavioral surcharge on our free acceptance in the Beloved."[18]

Inner Healed

Up until now, you may have noticed a few pot shots – or at least a bit of provoking language toward inner healing and deliverance mechanisms. Please understand that I am completely *for* inner healing. I even trained inner healing counselors for years. But there's a major difference in how I approach this subject. I am not trying to get people healed. I am convincing them that they *already* are healed.

It is not the end result but the *process itself*, which is problematic. Even the so-called "cross-centered" programs put the emphasis on you to "apply" the cross or the blood or some vision of Jesus or whatever to each and every area of your life like a magic fairy wand. It still leaves you to be the wizard wielding it, and thus the master of your own spirituality.

The fruit of a healthy emotional life comes from recognizing and believing that the old corrupt emotional life has been done away with. If a process is involved, it is only a process of recognizing something that has already taken place. We are not "peeling the onion" so to speak, through an endless removal of layer after layer of sin. Let's face the facts. The very *core* of that old

---

[18] Robert Capon, *The Foolishness of Preaching* (Grand Rapids: William B. Eerdmans Publishing, 1998), 32-33.

man was rotten to the very center. The whole onion needed to be thrown away. Instead, you have to see the process of maturation and Christian growth as one of opening your Christmas presents! You're not peeling back layers of garbage from 1982. You are plunging into the never-ending joy of discovery. Discovering the glorious gift that has been deposited within you.

Growth is Good

Christian growth and maturity is about *discovering* the True Self, not becoming it.

We completely affirm Christian *growth*. Even Jesus grew in wisdom and favor. We grow in lots of things. We are going from Glory to Glory. From light to light – *for in His light we see light* (Ps. 36:9). The expression of His faith is always growing in us. And primarily, we are growing in the renewal of the mind. What does that mean, to have the mind renewed? It is being continually awakened to the truth of what Christ has already accomplished. It is being renewed *to something*. And that "something" is a Reality that has already arrived.

We are realizing Him in us. We are realizing what He has done.

Many people who have learned to depend on inner healing therapy would feel that we are unnecessarily truncating the gospel. Oversimplifying. They feel comforted in the idea that God is progressively working on them. Makes them feel that He is ever present and near, and that He is concerned with their daily welfare on a continual basis. I would never want to take that away from anyone. He is Immanuel, God with us. You see we are not rejecting any of the experiential, daily participation with the presence of God. What we reject is the intent and nature of that participation. That God

83

comes in the guise of Freud or that He only shows up to scold us with negative attention. The role of Holy Spirit is not to snap on the rubber glove and give us a lifelong anal inspection. Holy Spirit's job is not quality control. As a Christian, Holy Spirit does not even come to *convict* you of sin! The scriptures say that He will convict the *world* of sin. You are no longer of this world. Conviction is a criminal courtroom term, used to indict a guilty offender of a crime (i.e. *You've been convicted!*). As a believer, we acknowledge that Jesus was convicted for us and took upon Himself our sentence. We are no longer motivated by a notion of guilt, but by the spirit of His kindness.

We must radically change the approach and perspective of our silly self-help programs. I know many people who are entrenched in inner healing and deliverance courses. Sure they are seeing a little bit of fruit, and that is great. It tells me that God is gracious and that He will use anything to woo people to Himself. But many are missing the whole point of the gospel and the end result will be devastating – a continual dependence on self-introspection and methodologies. Some don't even realize the co-dependence they are producing, as people are looking to the counselor or the *process itself* for their breakthrough.

People must realize that the Christian begins from the finish line. Robert Capon says brilliantly, "the flat announcement of the Gospel turned out to be that the saints were home before they started. God saves us single-handedly!"[19] We are already *inner healed*. Just turns out that most folks don't know it. It is all a completed work of grace.

---

[19] Robert Capon, *Between Noon and Three* (San Francisco: Harper & Row, 1982), 114-15.

Christian counseling is no more adept than secular psychology at pointing out roots of sin, past judgments, unforgiveness, abuses and reasons for generational problems. One does not have to be a believer to figure out that if dad beat you, then you are going to have anger issues. If mom was distant, you're going to have a disconnect with the opposite sex. Behavioral problems have roots in past woundedness. Anyone knows that.

Pointing out the root and reason for sin is really irrelevant at the end of the day. The antidote is always the same. We must reckon that the old self no longer exists. You couldn't pump up forgiveness for all those past hurts anyway. Your inability to forgive your parents was crucified with Christ.

The Curse is a Single Entity

If the cross of Christ need not be wielded like a magic wand on every individual hurt or mommy issue from the past, then the same is true for curses. We do not break our curses *one by one*.

When Christ died on the cross, He reversed an overarching, single entity called *the curse*. Individual sinful behaviors were not surgically dealt with on a case-by-case basis. The entire spirit of *sin itself* was demolished. Sin itself was a wicked governing force that was overthrown.

"Being joined to Him by faith, we have been freed from the *spirit of error* which dominated us – which caused us to be self-centered people. So the born-again person can never be, basically, self-centered again. You can move in a self-centered act. You can't be self-centered," says theological teacher Norman Grubb.[20]

Or consider George Swann's translation, "For when one has died, he has been freed from the *dominion* of sin" (Rom. 6:7, SWANN).

In other words, Christian growth is not a repeated process of *mortifying the flesh* as the old translators rendered Paul's statement to the Colossians. After telling them that the sinful nature has been circumcised away, he says, "*So treat as dead* your physical nature, as far as immorality, impurity, passion, evil desire, and greed are concerned" (Col. 3:5, GSPD). Treat the old man as it really is – *already* dead.

Another verse people like to misquote along these lines is Paul's admonition to "clean out the old leaven that you may be new." But the verse actually says:

> Cleanse out the old leaven that you may be a new lump, **as you really are unleavened.** For Christ, our Passover lamb, has been sacrificed (1 Cor. 5:7, ESV).

Paul says *you already are* free from the leaven of sin because of Christ. But the bottom line is that this verse is not even talking about cleaning out an *individual's soul*. Contextually, Paul was talking about removing a wicked person from the corporate church in Corinth who was a bad influence on other people. He was not telling them to purge themselves of individual sin, which is impossible. Only the blood of Christ can do that.

Realizing the New You

I have made the case that the renewal of the mind is the continual *remembrance* that you no longer live, but Christ lives in you. In fact, part of the renewal of the mind is to realize that you *already* have the mind of Christ! (1 Cor. 2:16) Even your mind is realizing that it is gloriously perfect.

Grubb points out that, as we mature, we realize an inability to accomplish the Christian life. As a newborn infant, you didn't much think about any of that. All you knew were a few basic principles. I know He died for me. I know my sins were forgiven. I know my father. And while I have an inner consciousness, I still view my relationship with God as an *exterior* one. I still assume that God and myself are living two separate existences as friendly neighbors who no longer feud.

"You regard it more as an external relationship. Life isn't an external relationship. Life is an internal relationship. Life isn't separation. It's union," says Grubb.[21] The fall caused us to think of everything in terms of *separation*. In the elementary state, I may think that it is *me* loving someone. But actually it is God's love permeating through me. He turned me into a lover.

As I mature, this faulty notion that I have an independent self apart from God begins to make itself evident. It is impossible for the *self* to overcome lust, depression, anger, etc. I may ask God for help, but I still have a concept that He is helping *me* to change *my* actions.

"Beware of asking God to help you," adds Grubb. "God doesn't help you to do a thing. He does it for you."

---

[21]Norman Grubb, "From Romans Seven to Romans Eight."

In the same way, the Romans 7 man strives to do what is right and finds it impossible. His assistance to God is rendered futile and defeating. By resisting the "flesh," he is actually affirming it. He is saying, "You exist! You exist!" He doesn't realize that there is nothing left about him that exists apart from Christ. The branch is in union with the vine. They are the same. You are not independent from Christ. You are one person. There is a realization that the self is not merely incapable of performing good. But in fact, self is *non-existent*. The independent self is a deception.

You are not an independent self, called to function in good. You are in *unio mystica*. The *"you"* has been replaced by *Christ*. Both the good and the evil of you have been replaced by the Tree of Life.

Cease resisting the old. You must rest in the *new*. Take no thought of how to overcome evil. Disregard altogether a sin consciousness. Let your eye be single. Full of light. In everything, see Christ alone. Don't look for devils behind every bush. View even temptation as a positive adventure, for by rejecting the false, you are confirming its opposite.

Spirit, Soul and Body

Let us dispel another common myth that can rob your joy. Those who would detract from your union with God often make the following claim. That your *spirit* becomes holy at salvation, but your *soul* is still in need of continual, lifelong work.

Inner healing and deliverance programs are all about purging the soul. Therapists have lengthy, intricate programs for soul cleansing, with reams of charts that detail all sorts of obscure imaginary demonic influences that will require extrication. Every one of these guys will tell you they don't rely on a formula, *but on the Holy Spirit.* They like the idea that they are more spiritually gifted than the average psychologist sans the master's degree. The "I rely on the Spirit" shtick also gives them plenty of room to add their own imaginary demonic influences to the aforementioned list. Each of these amateur exorcists has really thrown their identity into their role as Christ's vicar in the counseling room, so you have to be super careful not to invalidate them, even though most of their methods are baloney. It is futile to engage them in a discussion on the finished work of Christ, because each one will always point to their experience as the proof text, rather than their Bible. They will always refer to a case where someone screamed or vomited something up in their session. My children scream and vomit at the amusement park, but that doesn't mean a real Christian has demons.

Ye cannot drink the cup of the Lord, and the cup of devils: ye cannot be partakers of the Lord's table, and of the table of devils (1 Cor. 10:21, KJV).

Wonder what the word "cannot" means in the verse above? Simple. It means it is *impossible* to have God and the devil at the same time.

Again, please don't misunderstand – I *love* inner healing and deliverance – but I simply believe that Jesus has inner healed and delivered me. Don't complicate it.

People who hold to this "dirty soul/clean spirit" concept have scant Bible to back it up. It puts your "spirit" somewhere out in an untouchable, imaginary outer space that you will never touch, taste or handle in reality. They love the term "positional." They say that *positionally* you are holy, but it will take a long time (think

120 years) to *appropriate* it into your soul. In empirical reality, you will always be a dirty soulish person.

We were once joking about this silly notion, together with renowned Mozambiquan missionary Roland Baker saying, "Oh, if only I could meet my *spirit* man! Yes, I hear that my spirit man is a really nice guy. He's so holy. My spirit man and my soul man should get together for tea sometime. My soul could really learn a thing or two from him."

Baker is an incredible theological mind and extraordinary missionary who has planted thousands of churches in Africa with his well-known wife, Heidi. In conversation, he explained how all throughout the Old and New Testament, the words "spirit" and "soul" are used *interchangeably*. It is the religious mind that has tried to carve them apart. But if the soul is just as clean as the rest of you, this has a devastating effect to our old-school notion of inner healing.

Entire Sanctification

There is only one scripture that could remotely indicate that man is a tripartite being, made up of three parts: spirit, soul and body.

May God Himself, the God of peace, sanctify you through and through. May your whole spirit, soul and body be kept blameless at the coming of our Lord Jesus Christ. The one who calls you is faithful and He will do it (1 Thess. 5:23,24 NIV).

Paul is not going into a big clinical dissection of the human composition here. It is simply a closing benediction at the very end of his letter. This term "spirit, soul and body" should be taken loosely as to indicate the *entire being*. In the same way, Christ spoke of loving

God with all your *soul, mind, heart and strength*. Why didn't we divide the anatomy of man into these four parts? Elsewhere, Christ mentions only three of these components – soul, heart and mind – but failing to include *strength*. The inconsistency shows He didn't intend to make a strict vivisection of the human into four unique parts. He just meant to love God with your *entire being* (Luke 10:27; Matt. 22:37).

Unfortunately, we have in this case a massive theological paradigm forming around a single verse of scripture. Whether we have three clinically delineated parts, I don't really know. And guess what? I really don't care! If the apostles thought this an important subject, why didn't they ever talk about it? Paul does say the word is able to "divide spirit and soul," but he says that in a poetic, allegorical sense, not a theological one (Heb. 4:12). We must be careful of eisegetical interpretation here (imposing one's preconceived ideas into the text). The traditional Christian view held by the majority of lay people and theologians worldwide – both past and present – is that man is a *bipartite* creature made of two components: material (body/flesh) and spiritual (soul/spirit). The three-pronged theory wasn't popular until the days of Watchman Nee and others.

The danger does not come so much from building a theology on one single verse (although that's dangerous enough). The danger comes from building yet *another* theology *on top* of the theology that was built on the single verse: *Now that I believe I am three parts, I will further believe that salvation only applies to only one of those parts. My spirit is the holy part, my soul is dirty and my body is way down the ladder!*

Over time, we have built an entire system on this little verse that is like a crumbling, inverted pyramid. It is bound to fall over. What if the human personhood is far

91

more complex than one, two, three or even a thousand parts? Just as the human body is made anatomically of innumerable parts, what if the unseen part of you is equally as intricate? Luke 17:21 says you have the entire Kingdom within you. The Bridegroom calls you as beautiful as Tirzah – saying you are like an entire *City of Delight* (Song of Sol. 6:4). Zechariah speaks typologically of you, the New Jerusalem, saying you are so expansive that you are like a city without walls (Zech. 2:2-4). What if the inside of you is far bigger than the outside? The unseen realm may be vastly different than we have supposed. Adam Clarke says that a believer is a "little world in himself."[22]

To say that one's perfection applies only to the "spirit man" while attesting that the soul is still dirty and in need of purging, presents a number of problems. Foremost, is the quandary that the spirit and soul are *still conjoined*. Even a tripartite theologian would not utterly cut off the spirit from the soul – just as to split the bone from marrow would indisputably result in the death of a man. For a man to be alive, his soul and spirit must surely be intertwined just as the soul and body are intrinsically connected. A body without a spirit is a corpse. A soul without a body is a specter.

Assuming hypothetically then that our soul and spirit are two parts, but indeed interconnected, how then would light dwell within the confines of darkness? Is a spirit truly pure if it is still connected to a filthy soul? Is truth really truth when it is laced with error? How would sweet water be couched in a poisoned vessel?

The demarcation of spirit, soul and body does not seem to be the intent of the Apostle Paul, else he

---

[22] Clarke, *Commentary on the Whole Bible*, Excerpt from 2 Cor. 17.

would have focused more thoroughly and coherently on the subject. Paul was a masterful logician and would not have left such an important subject veiled, if indeed it was so important to compartmentalize the inner man.

Completely Set Apart

I want to return to the aforementioned verse in question. I intentionally included what I consider to be a terrible translation of it – but I found it to be poorly translated in almost every Bible version I read. Therefore, I translated it myself. It is the primary verse used to suggest that the *soul* has to be progressively sanctified.

May God Himself, the God of peace, sanctify you through and through. May your whole spirit, soul and body be kept blameless at the coming of our Lord Jesus Christ. The one who calls you is faithful and He will do it (1 Thess. 5:23-24 NIV).

Sounds like a prayer for something that hasn't happened yet, doesn't it? Now here's where theologians put Frankenstein together in the back rooms of their eisegetical laboratories.

For starters, translators added the word "may" to make this sound like a request. *May God please clean you up.* Also, the word for "sanctify" here is aorist, meaning you can't honestly specify whether it is repeated, continuous, instantaneous, past or accomplished. In other words, this verse in no way indicates that your sanctification is an ongoing process. It could very well just say "God sanctifies." In addition, Paul is not speaking to an individual "you" composed of three parts. He doesn't suggest that each part of "you" needs to be saved. He is speaking corporately to "you all" (*umas*), the same Greek word Jesus used when He said, "Come after me, and I will make you fishers of men" (Matt. 4:19).[23] Remember, he's closing a letter to the corporate group. Finally, Paul speaks of God *preserving* you. This is the real kicker that knocks the dirty soul idea out of the bucket. The word "be preserved" or *tereo* indicates that something has *already taken place* on this side of Christ's return.[24] Perfection is not coming, but has already been given. Therefore it is preserved. You do not preserve something that you don't already have. Furthermore, Paul says it is *God* who guards over it until the end, not you.

After correcting all of these misconceptions, I feel that it actually says something along these lines:

> *And Himself, the God of peace, is the one who sets all of you apart completely. Your whole spirit, soul and body is preserved blameless until the coming of our Lord Jesus Christ. The one who calls you is faithful and He will preserve you.*

This is a verse that affirms perfection not filthiness! It attests to your union with God. Some would argue that we are splitting ontological hairs. Why are you getting distracted with Greek syntax Crowder? Why focus on the jot and tittle? Tell us more miracle stories of levitation and stigmatas! Enough with the grammar lessons!

What I am telling you here is one of the most revolutionary principles in Christendom. I am preaching reformation clearer than it was preached 500 years ago. Martin Luther, you didn't go far enough. God didn't just cover your sins; He erased *sinfulness* from you. Jesus saved *you*. Not some invisible, hidden, intangible part

---

[23] Strong, *Exhaustive Concordance of the Bible*, Entry 5209.

[24] Strong, *Exhaustive Concordance of the Bible*, Entry 5083.

of you. He saved you completely. A complete sacrifice for a complete salvation.

Miracles are pointless if I am working them to induct people into a do-it-yourself religion.

Adam Clarke says of this complete salvation, "But if man be not perfectly saved from all sin, sin does triumph, and satan exult, because they have done a mischief that Christ either cannot or will not remove."[25]

Strong, Undiluted Grace

Had the reformers thought these elements through a bit more, I do think they would have been persuaded. John Calvin, for instance, clearly said that sanctification stemmed from *Christ's* cross and was not distinctly different from one's initial justification at salvation:

> *Do you wish, then to attain righteousness in Christ? You must first possess Christ; but you cannot possess Him without being made partaker in His sanctification, because He cannot be divided into pieces. Since, therefore, it is solely by expending Himself that the Lord gives us these benefits to enjoy, He bestows* **both of them at the same time, the one never without the other.** *Thus it is clear how true it is that we are justified not without works yet not through works, since in our sharing in Christ, which justifies us,* **sanctification is just as much included as righteousness.**[26]

How can we separate our justification from our sanctification? These salvific benefits are inseparable, for they

---

[25] Clarke, "Entire Sanctification."

[26] Calvin, *Institutes,* 3.16.1 p. 797-798.

are both rooted in our union with Christ. I hope you're beginning to realize how scandalous all of this is. Do you think John Crowder is offensive because of silly antics or strange miracles? Let me tell you the real root of offense dear friend. The glorious bliss of Christ's cross spills out of us every which way but loose. Its freedom and life affect us on every level. People may not realize it. They may get hung up on our shock language or comedic manifestations. But at the end of the day, it is the cross that scandalizes them.

Are you ready for the drunken melee of reformation? This revelation of God's grace is the single strong drink to fuel it. This revelation of co-crucifixion is the core of my union and the source of my continual holy intoxication. My *soul* is drunk on the fatness of His house! Let us return to those brilliant words of Robert Capon:

The Reformation was a time when men went blind, staggering drunk because they had discovered, in the dusty basement of late medievalism, a whole cellar full of fifteen-hundred-year-old, two-hundred-proof grace—of bottle after bottle of pure distillate of Scripture, one sip of which would convince anyone that God saves us single-handedly. The word of the gospel—after all those centuries of trying to lift yourself into Heaven by worrying about the perfection of your bootstraps—suddenly turned out to be a flat announcement that the saved were home before they started...Grace has to be drunk straight: no water, no ice, and certainly no ginger ale; neither goodness, nor badness, nor the flowers that bloom in the spring of super spirituality could be allowed to enter into the case.[27]

---

[27] Capon, *Between Noon and Three*, 114-15.

Paul was a man who walked the Earth *out of his mind*. Regularly engaged in ecstatic encounters throughout the New Testament, he experienced continually the transcendent Glory of his union with Christ.

Called insane, a fool and even a madman, Paul was tasting an otherworldly reality that had transformed his entire existence. The Roman governor Festus called him a raving lunatic:

> *That was too much for Festus. He interrupted with a shout: "Paul, you're crazy! You've read too many books, spent too much time staring off into space! Get a grip on yourself, get back in the real world!"* (Acts 26:14, MSG)

For the apostle, I believe that the message of regeneration and mystical union with God were all one in the same. Paul said in a thousand and a thousand ways the same primary revelation of what happened to us at the cross. It was a message of a *new creation* in Christ. All of his joys, all of the marvels he performed, all of his ecstasies found their source in this one revelation of what Christ's cross had accomplished.

Some think that ecstasies and sweet contemplative experiences with the Lord draw us closer to Him. But this is a mistake. We have these experiences because we are *already* united with Him. The unity happened on His tree. Now, our experiences are a remarkable by-product.

We must pay close attention to the gospel Paul preached. Paul felt a special ownership of the message he carried – even going so far as to call it *my gospel*.

Without batting an eyelash, he made about the boldest statement a human being could make:

> *The ultimate reckoning will come when God evaluates every person through Jesus Christ in accordance with **my interpretation** of the good news* (Rom. 2:16, BCJ).

On Judgment Day, everybody's fate will be filtered through Paul's interpretation! Consider the following:

- Paul wrote two-thirds of the New Testament.
- Paul's letters were the first inspired writings of the early church. Written and distributed *before* the books of Matthew, Mark, Luke and John.
- Mark traveled with and learned from Paul *prior* to writing the Book of Mark.
- Luke traveled with and learned from Paul *prior* to writing the Book of Luke.
- Luke freely admits that he was not an eyewitness to the Book of Luke – but Paul did influence him.
- Luke learned the ropes from Paul before writing the Book of Acts.
- The Book of Acts is largely centered on Paul, who quickly takes front and center stage.
- Scholars such as Robert Capon state, "The Gospels, accordingly, were written for the sake of the Epistles, not the other way around."[28]
- Paul had to bring correction to keep Peter in line with the gospel.
- Peter makes a point to specifically affirm and validate the letters of Paul.
- Even men sent from James were not living in accordance to the same message Paul carried.

---

[28] Capon, *Health, Money & Love and Why We Don't Enjoy Them*, 32.

NEW CREATION REALITIES

In fact, the Lord used Paul to lay the very core foundational revelation of the cross in the New Testament.

It is impossible to understand the book of James without filtering it through the gospel Paul preaches. You will *really* get tweaked out if you read James backwards! It takes careful study of James to see that his connection between faith and works is not in opposition to Paul's. Instead, he is focusing on different aspects of a believer's life. James was really more of a transition book for Jews in Jerusalem than it was a clear articulation of New Covenant grace.

The radical thing about the message God deposited into Paul was that *God Himself deposited it!* After Judas hung himself, the apostles figured they would find a replacement for him. They prayed. They fasted. They tried numerous things. Finally, they just rolled a dice! They appointed Matthias to replace him. But do you remember ever hearing about Matthias again after that?

What if God had His own selection for a replacement? Paul said, "I was not appointed by any group of people or any human authority, but by Jesus Christ Himself and by God the Father, who raised Jesus from the dead" (Gal. 1:1, NLT). And the Lord gave his revelation directly to him, "for I would have you know, brethren, that the gospel which was preached by me is not according to man. For I neither received it from man, nor was I taught it, but I received it through a revelation of Jesus Christ" (Gal. 1:11-12, NASB). In fact, Paul – like Christ Himself – did not minister under any human authority. He received the word of God and, "when this happened, I did not rush out to consult with any human being" (Gal. 1:16, NLT).

Now my intent is not to idolize Paul the way some Catholics would idolize Mary. I merely suggest that there is a core revelation that was entrusted to this man that is imperative for the church to take hold of. We have to see the entire Bible through Pauline eyes. It is the message of grace. A message of righteousness that comes through *trusting*, not from striving or contending. Furthermore, it is a message that the cross does more than forgive sins. It eradicates the *inward propensity toward sin*. It does not put you on a road toward union with God. It accomplishes that union in one ultimate stroke. This is the scandal.

Scholar C.T. Wood writes:

> *Here it must suffice to insist on the fact that (Paul's) religion and all his theology are based on his daily experience of mystic union with Christ: this is the clue to the true interpretation of his language. Finally, this also explains what is a rather startling fact about his Epistles, namely, the paucity of his references to the sayings and deeds of Jesus on Earth, other than the Crucifixion and Resurrection. ... The fact is that he was preoccupied with the daily presence of the Risen Lord. Historical Christianity was to him the basis on which this communion rested; but it faded into the background before the present reality.*[29]

Paul the Ecstatic

This core message of a glorious, happy union with God was the source of Paul's supernaturally crazy joy. Joy is not just a substance or an emotion – it is a *person*. Christ has become our inexhaustible joy. Living in this

---

[29] Wood, *The Life, Letters and Religion of St. Paul*, 75.

thrilling realm of union, Paul records numerous ecstatic, or *ekstasis* experiences that marked his lifestyle. This means that Paul was "standing outside of himself" continually in the realm of the spirit. Tranced out as an effect of faith expressing itself through love. He was filled and possessed by Holy Spirit. This seemed rather unusual to the onlooker.

Paul's joy was rooted in his absolute uprightness before the sight of God. He says that everyone will appear before the judgment seat of Christ, and all will have to pay the piper. "Yet my uprightness is manifest in the sight of God," says Paul, attesting to the imputed righteousness of Christ on that day (2 Cor. 5:11, CON). Does this sound crazy? Crazy indeed.

"Are these wild words?" he asks.

"If I be mad, it is for God's cause," continues Paul (2 Cor. 5:13, CON). Or as the Taylor translation puts it, "Are we insane to say such things about ourselves? If so, it is to bring Glory to God" (2 Cor. 5:13, TAY). This new relationship of perfect union produces a stupefying, indescribable ecstasy in the heart and mind of the believer. For this reason, Paul has to explain his unorthodox insensibility.

If my enthusiasm makes me seem, as my critics say, "a bit mad", it is for God's honour; if on the other hand I display any worldly wisdom, it is for your benefit (2 Cor. 12:13, WAND).

"If we are standing outside ourselves in ecstasy, it is for God; if we are just being normal, it is for your sake," he says in the Ben Campbell Johnson translation. If I'm drunk on faith and love – *blame God!* But if instead I appear "sober," as the King James puts it, it's just so that I can explain this stuff to you guys!

Try as he may, Paul labored his entire life to put this glorious revelation of the cross into words. It was this deep, spiritual apprehension of the gospel that was likely imparted to him in his encounter in Paradise. He writes:

> *Fourteen years ago I was the subject of an incom-prehensible ecstasy, in which truths too great for human language were imparted to me* (1 Cor. 12:1, GBS).

For Paul, the euphoria of the cross had taken a spiritual ownership of him, and he of it. He was prohibited from considering anything else. After explaining his madness, he continues his dialogue by saying that *the love of Christ compels us* (2 Cor. 5:14). This word for "compel" or "constrain" literally means that he was overmastered and pressed upon every side by love. He was *possessed* by love. He was a *love slave*.

And how was he now owned and occupied by love?

> *Because we are of the opinion that if one was put to death for all, then all have undergone death* (2 Cor. 5:14, BAS).

The death of Christ was not a mere legal exchange that got you off the hook. You're not a crook that got away with something due to a legal loophole. It was a mysti-cally transformative event that *changed* you from a crook to a model citizen.

> *His purpose in dying for all was that men, while still in life, should cease to live for themselves, and should live for Him who for their sake died and was raised to life* (2 Cor. 5:15, NEB).

You're Not Human Anymore

Looking at the previous line of discussion, we should not make the following mistake. Paul was not merely stimulated by Jesus' model of self-sacrifice, and therefore choosing to make a change in his own personal lifestyle. Jesus' death was not simply a model for Paul to follow. Rather, it was a supernatural transaction that altered the core *substance* of the believer. This word "substance" has been the subject of massive theological splits and divisions in church history. It is a very important word and I don't use it lightly.

You have been mystically changed from one *substance* into another. You have a different *essence* about you now.

Jesus did not just come as a moral reformer, giving us a life to imitate. Rather, He substituted His very *God-DNA* into our own. It is as if a chemical reaction went off in a laboratory. Although you still have a body of flesh, you are *not merely human anymore*.

Does this statement offend you? Don't worry. We're not going to put tin foil antennae on our heads and start an alien cult! But it is true that you are now from *another world!* You are born of Heaven. Paul continues his 2 Corinthians 5 dialogue with this profound assertion:

Therefore for the future we know no one simply as a man (2 Cor. 5:16a, WEY).

And therefore, henceforward, we do not think of anybody in a merely human fashion (2 Cor. 5:16, KNOX).

You no longer have this excuse to sin: *Well, I'm only human.* The flat announcement of the gospel is that you are *not* human. You are no longer an Adamite. You are now *sons of God*. Just as Christ was a man, yet *more than a man*, so are you in this world (1 John 4:17).

> *Even if we have known Christ simply as a man, yet now we do so no longer* (2 Cor. 5:16b, WEY).

> *Once, I mistakenly thought of Christ that way, merely as a human being like myself. How differently I feel now!* (2 Cor. 5:16, TAY)

Perhaps we would be more correct, in fact, to say that now you are *truly* human. As a result of the fall of Adam, mankind became "less than human," in that we had fallen away from the original image that God had created. Now, you have been restored to the original design of humanity. But it goes further still. Your relationship with God is now *better* than Eden. If Adam walked with God in the cool of the day, then you can now boast that God walks *inside* of you. Not until the cross of Christ was man allowed to have the permanent *indwelling* presence of God.

The union of God with humanity is seen most clearly in the incarnation. In Christ, humanity and divinity see their full reconciliation.

Neos vs. Kainos

So what is the product of this transformation? If I am no longer human in the way that I once was, then what have I become? Consider the next verse, 2 Cor. 5:17 in the following translations:

> *Therefore, if any one is in* **union with Christ***, he is a* **new being** (TCNT)

*Whosoever, then, is in Christ, is a **new creation*** (CON)

*... he becomes a **new person altogether*** (PHI)

You are literally *little christs* – that's what the word "Christian" means. Little *anointed ones*. God carriers. If you're into alien movies, consider yourself a *host*.

The verse continues to read, "his old life has disappeared, everything has become new about him" (KNOX). And also, "old things are passed away; behold, all things are become new" (KJV). Numerous versions even suggest that "he is in a *new world*" (BAS). We will explain this a bit later.

For starters, you should realize that Christ did not just give you a fresh start at the *old you*. You are not just a remodeled version, nor did He just give you a second chance at the old Adamic self. You've been thoroughly *replaced* with something fresh.

Understand that there are a number of different Greek terms for the word "new" in the letters of Paul. One of these words is *neos*. The word "neos" suggests that something is new in relation to *time*.[30]

I had an old Volkswagen. It broke down. Now I have a new (neos) Volkswagen.

I had an old pair of Adidas. Those shoes wore out. Now I have a new (neos) pair of Adidas.

New in the aforementioned senses concerns antiquity versus modernity. The new Adidas are in every respect

---

[30] Strong, *Exhaustive Concordance of the Bible*, Entry 3501.

just the same as the old ones, but I just bought them clean and sparkly. *Neos* speaks of a timeframe. Young versus aged. This, however, is certainly *not* what the apostle was saying when he called you a *new creation*. You are not new according to *time*. You are not just a later model of the same old Volkswagen that you were before. You are something altogether *different* than you were before. I will attempt to explain.

Contrary to popular opinion, the gospel is not a "second chance" message (i.e. I botched my life, but God forgave me and gave me a *new* start). He didn't just give you a new start at the same ordinary human self. That is not really good news! If I botched it the first time, what is to prevent me from botching it again? Jesus didn't just forgive you, clean the slate and give you another chance to perform better. Instead, He transformed the very *substance* of what you were.

There is another word for *new* that the writer uses in this passage. It is the word "kainos." *Kainos* is a different kind of "new." It means new in *quality*. It means unique. It means novel. It is something never seen before – unusual and innovative. It is a new kind of substance.[31]

"Wow! Never seen that before. That's *new!*"

You are a *kainos* creation. The Earth has not yet beheld what you are. You have not begun to scratch the surface of what your new super suit can do! If you had an old Volkswagen, you don't just get an updated model of another Volkswagen. Instead, you are now driving the USS Enterprise! You had an old pair of Adidas, but now you have a kainos pair of shoes that

---

[31] Strong, *Exhaustive Concordance of the Bible*, Entry 2537.

make you levitate, walk through walls, turn invisible and shoot hundred dollar bills out the tongue! You are a *new breed*.

Seeing the Greek perspective on the word "new" changes everything in understanding the difference between the old and new self. Furthermore, the nature of the word "kainos" is special in that it is a *corporate* word. It speaks not in terms of an old individual self being replaced by a new individual self. Instead it infers that you are grafted into a bigger picture. You have been united with a larger corporate entity. You have been brought into a *whole new world*.

A Whole New World

In your new world, all you see is Jesus. Devils may exist, but not in your realm. The cross for us has not just become tunnel vision. Instead, it is the lens through which we see the world. Everything is Christ. Norman Grubb went so far as to say he didn't even see devils anymore, just *God in disguise*.

You can see Christ in all and through all. Your eye is single. Now everything you touch, taste and see screams *Christ!* You have transitioned out of the old world and into the Kingdom of Heaven. Although you are walking the Earth and sitting on a bench next to an unbeliever, the two of you are actually dwelling in two completely different dimensions. One is in Heaven; the other is in hell – yet you're on the same bench. Paul said, "May I never boast except in the cross of our Lord Jesus Christ, through which *the world has been crucified to me, and I to the world*. Neither circumcision nor uncircumcision means anything; *what counts is a new creation*" (Gal. 6:14-15, NIV).

You see it was not just *you* who died on that tree. The whole world was crucified to you!

The old era that was represented by Adam and the fall of humanity has been replaced by the new era of Christ and His Kingdom. You are in a whole new realm now. You are grafted into something bigger than yourself. You are one with God.

God did not just add the new you on top of the old you. He *replaced* the old version with the new version, just as He replaced the old era with the new era. I often teach this concept in tandem with my friend Benjamin Dunn, who expands on the word kainos thoroughly in his book *The Happy Gospel*.

"Everything we were 'in Adam' has been shattered and destroyed! We have been completely disconnected from the fallen state of humanity and its curse, which is separation from God, and have entered into a new world altogether," writes Dunn. "When we came to Christ we entered into a new era – the era of Christ the Last Adam."[32]

Furthermore, Dunn quotes an incredibly well researched book on this subject, the *Dictionary of Paul and His Letters*:

> The translation "old self" and "new self" is too individualistic, since the idea certainly means the individual Christian. ... The "old person" is not just the sin nature, which was judged at the cross and to which is added a "new person." The "old person" is what believers were "in Adam" (in the old era). The "old" points to everything connected with the fall of

---

[32] Dunn, *The Happy Gospel*, 66.

humanity and with the subjection to the distress and death of a transitory life, separated from God.[33]

You are now living a new and marvelous supernatural existence. Let us look at the Heinz Cassirer translation of Romans 6:4:

*Well then, by virtue of undergoing baptism into death we were buried with Him, in order that, as Christ was raised from the dead by the Father's glorious power, we, too, might live and move in a **new kind of existence** (CAS).*

Or as J.B. Phillips translates it, you "rise to life on a new plane altogether" (PHI). You are now sharing Jesus' relationship with the Father.

He died once for all to end sin's power, but now He lives forever in unbroken fellowship with God (Rom. 6:10, TAY).

For His death was a unique event that need not be repeated; but His life, he keeps on living for God (Rom. 6:10, CJB).

Deity Nature

Here is another way to describe the transition that has taken place. We have discussed how the vast majority of the church wrongly believes that the new nature was *added on* to the old nature – assuming this to be the battle depicted in Romans 7. They think that the old must be wrestled down by the new to reach Romans 8 – the full manifestation of mature sonship.

---

[33] Hawthorne, Martin and Reid, *Dictionary of Paul and His Letters*, 628.

Another – albeit minority – group of Christians take the route popularized by John and Charles Wesley, John Fletcher and others. They would be termed "holiness movement" people. They're known for terms such as "entire sanctification," "sinless perfection," etc. This group is often considered suspect or a bit off course, but they're actually a bit closer to the truth.

The holiness group maintains that there is a "second work of grace" after salvation, in which the old nature is supernaturally eradicated and replaced with a new one. To them, *sanctification* happens in this once-off type of spirit baptism.

Neither of these theologies is what we advocate. The new does *replace* the old. It is no mere addition. The holiness folks do have a partial truth. But the replacement does not occur in some elusive *second work*. It happened on Christ's cross, and it occurs at salvation.

If we really want to take things a step further, there is a third option. Norman Grubb makes the case that humans have *no nature*. That is, we have no independent nature outside of our dominating entity. We are simply containers that take on the attributes of our controlling deity. Either Christ lives in us, or satan.

"In every case, a temple is only the dwelling place of a deity and reveals his presence, not its own. We are either a temple that contains an idol god, or one in which the living God dwells and walks. A temple has no nature but that of the god in it," writes Grubb.

Grubb contends that there are really only two options here. We are temples owned and occupied by one of two forces. Before we were saved, we are aware that we were owned by sin. But the problem was deeper than "you were a sinner." By living a lie, by default you were *sin itself.* Take it even further and you hit a truth that perhaps you couldn't quite stomach until now. You were *satan.* By demanding a false existence, you were a de facto child of your father the devil. But that was never your true, original DNA. Your true identity, even before the fall of Adam, is found in the image of God.

Just as Jesus said that He and His Father are one – in the same way, the son always embodies his father. In your unredeemed state – as the *old man* – you were an embodiment of satan. Perhaps that satanic nature had not fully manifested to the degree it did in an Adolf Hitler or a Charles Manson. But nevertheless, it was there. Apart from a revelation of Christ, all is depravity.

There is no question of *partial* depravity. You were completely darkened and dead in your sins. But in Christ, the exact opposite is true. You are complete *light in the Lord.* Now Christ is walking about *as you.* You are now an embodiment of your true Father God, in the image of your Elder Brother.

Free From the Curse

A few decades ago, as the charismatic church individuated from its predecessor, the Pentecostal movement, one of the elements of focus became *spiritual warfare.* I believe that this was a God-breathed thing in many ways, because prior to this, the Western church was largely unaware of the unseen realm. There was a naturalistic bent not even to believe in demons, angels or spiritual things. I do believe that the Lord wanted people to be aware of the reality of the spiritual realm.

This emphasis on warfare and the demonic served its purpose in many ways. But along with it came a number of extremes, as well as a de-emphasis on the new creation realities afforded us at the cross. There is a faulty assumption that union is something we progressively climb into, rather than a state we begin with at salvation.

Today, your average deliverance or inner healing guru has reams upon reams of scientifically categorized demons, unclean spirits, generational curses and various imps and goblins that you need to take care of. They love to be experts on "the deep things of satan." Most advocate that it is an individual believer's task to go through these curses and renounce them one by one. Often they even want you to repent for things you didn't even do, *just in case*. They want you to repent for atrocities committed hundreds of years ago that you had no participation in whatsoever. It makes them feel spiritual to invent strange and obscurely named demons, attaching some kind of historical reference to each one for validity. They enjoy digging around and navel gazing in an introspective spiral that never really has an end in sight to all the soulish cleanup they expect of you.

Do not be lured away from the simplicity of the gospel. Jesus does not expect you to break your curses *one-by-one*. If it is your job to go through and break every generational sin, it's going to take you a long time! You'll keep your deliverance counselor in business indefinitely. You will have to repent for your daddy's sin, then for your great-granddaddy's Pabst Blue Ribbon drinking addiction, then your great-great-great grandmammy's snuff chewing addiction and so on and so forth. In fact, you will need to repent all the way back to great-great-great-great-great-great granddaddy Adam. I don't think ancestry.com will trace your family tree back that far.

Or, you can believe that the *Last Adam* came and severed sin at the root.

You can believe that in Christ, on the cross, something called "the" curse was broken. The entire fallenness of the Adamic era found its conclusion on Calvary. That entire, governing, dominating entity called *sin itself* was eradicated. The very thing that evidenced your dissolved union with God was abolished, putting you back into permanent, unbroken fellowship with Him.

Breaking your curses one-by-one is a subtle form of works. People use crafty language to draw you into this. "Yes, of course the blood of Jesus is enough. But you have to *apply* the blood to each thing." They say that you must "appropriate" what Jesus has done. You must "position" yourself for it. You must "yield" to it.

Nobody will give you straight language. They are really advocating that you *work* for your holiness. Not with outward observances of course, but with inward straining and groaning. In other words, you must count on your *willpower.*

Wasn't Paul Still Pressing in for Perfection?

I've made an extensive argument that no effort of your own will bring you into perfection. This is where most scholars misconstrue the words of Paul. Surely, they say, Paul did not claim to be perfect. Wasn't he pressing on to perfection? Wasn't he still contending for it?

> Not that I have already attained, **or am already perfected**; but I press on, that I may lay hold of that for which Christ Jesus has also laid hold of me (Phil. 3:12, NKJV).

This passage is usually taken out of context as a snapshot. Only a few verses prior to this, Paul claims that his own labors toward right standing with God were nothing but "dung." Why would he say his entire pressing towards perfection amounted to a pile of poop ... and therefore, his goal is to now continue pressing in and crank out more poop?

Let's read this in a bit more context to see what Paul is actually "pressing in" for. He warns the Philippians about the religionists in this chapter, the "mutilators of the flesh," and says he was once a zealous Pharisee just like them:

> But whatever was to my profit I now consider loss for the sake of Christ. What is more, I consider everything a loss compared to the surpassing greatness of knowing Christ Jesus my Lord, for whose sake I have lost all things. I consider them rubbish (lit. poop), that I may gain Christ and be found in him, not having a righteousness of my own that comes from the law, but that which is through faith in Christ—the righteousness that comes from God and is by faith. I want to know Christ and the power of His resurrection and the fellowship of sharing in His sufferings, **becoming like him in His death, and so, somehow, to attain to the resurrection from the dead.** Not that I have already obtained all this, or have already been made perfect, but I press on to take hold of that for which Christ Jesus took hold of me (Phil. 3:7-12, NIV).

Folks love to insert their opinion on this passage. But let's just take a stark naked, cold shower look at what Paul is literally saying here. He says that he wants to *be killed and raised from the dead.*

Whose brain waves work like that? Who is walking around, making a life goal of that sort of craziness?

College Prep Instructor: *Paul, do you have any ambitions, any long-term achievements you wanna accom-*

plish? What are your career goals? Dreams for the future kind of thing ...

Paul: *Well doc, I'm obsessed with this idea of getting brutally murdered and then standing back up on my own two feet again. Just can't shake the thought of it.*

Paul says nothing about pressing on for sanctification or moral perfection in this passage. He says just the opposite on those grounds. Instead, he's pushing for something a little creepier – toward his "high calling" of martyrdom. This was not a salvation or personal holiness issue – let's get inside his head for a second here. As crazy as it sounds, Paul was looking forward to literally, physically taking a bullet for Jesus. In saying that he was not "already perfected," this can better be translated as I am not "already at the goal" (AAT). It's also the word for "completed" or "consummated." You have to put this into context. Re-read this chapter and you will understand. Paul was not asserting a lack of moral perfection (though he acknowledges that he could not perfect himself through legalistic righteousness). Paul consistently boasts in the perfecting work of Christ.

Paul wanted to experience everything that salvation by the blood of Christ offered him. But here, he is literally stating that he has not yet reached his ultimate goal of *martyrdom for the faith*!

"Christ died, not only as a victim for sin, but as a martyr to the truth. ... as a martyr to the truth, St. Paul wished to imitate Him. Not only in the apostle, but in the primitive Christians generally, there seems to have been a strong desire after martyrdom," writes commentator Dr. Adam Clarke, adding that Paul's statement about not being perfect literally means, "I am not yet crowned, in consequence of having suffered martyrdom. I am quite satisfied that the apostle here alludes to the Olympic games, and the word teteleiwmai is the proof; for teleiwqhnai is spoken of those who have completed their race, reached the goal, and are honoured with the prize."[34]

The Philippians would have understood this Olympic game language completely. One who finished a race was "perfect" and is where we get our term "martyr." Clarke has done his homework. Knowing this is an often misunderstood verse, his commentary points to ancient theologians such as Philo, Clement of Alexandria, Basil the Great, Eusebius and Balsamon in their use of the word *perfection* here as it refers to receiving the crown of martyrdom:

> *St. Paul, therefore, is not speaking here of any deficiency in his own grace, or spiritual state; he does not mean by not being yet perfect, that he had a body of sin and death cleaving to him, and was still polluted with indwelling sin, as some have most falsely and dangerously imagined; he speaks of his not having terminated his course by martyrdom, which he knew would sooner or later be the case. This he considered as the teleiwsiv, or perfection, of his whole career, and was led to view every thing as imperfect or unfinished till this had taken place.*[35]

Furthermore, it is not even by Paul's own ability that he "presses toward" or accomplishes his goal, but it is "the power that enables (Christ)" which "will transform our lowly bodies so that they will be like his glorious body" (verse 21).

---

[34] Clarke, *Commentary on the Whole Bible*, Excerpt from Phil. 3.
[35] Clarke, *Commentary on the Whole Bible*, Excerpt from Phil. 3.

Changing our Language

Modern Christianity is chock full of bite-sized, cliché words that refer to completely unbiblical concepts. There is a prevailing *language of unbelief* in the church. Most of the church is still in an Old Covenant, do-it-yourself perspective. When people today talk about "pressing in" they refer to somehow obtaining "more of God" or "getting into God's Glory." It is sacrilege to believe God could give you anything *more* than the fullness of Himself on the cross. It is also sacrilege to think there's something you could do to "position" yourself to get into His Glory. Jesus positioned *Himself* to get you into the Glory.

It is imperative that we change our language in light of the gospel. We must make it a goal to rid ourselves of anti-gospel terminology that permeates the vocabulary of the church. Stop speaking as if we lack something.

You will never hear us talk about *having a flesh day*, or *overcoming the flesh*. This is a dead language for the believer. Stop speaking that way. You don't have a "flesh" anymore in the naughty sense. That is a language of works and paganism.

I'm not *pressing in* anymore. I've been pressed into.
I'm not *contending* anymore. I've been contended for.
I'm not a *God chaser* anymore. I've been chased down, roped, hogtied, bagged and dragged.
I'm not *appropriating* what I have. It's mine.
I'm not *getting closer* to God. He's like a Siamese twin.
I'm not even *seeking God* anymore. He found me.

Stop Seeking God

You will never hear us talk to believers about *seeking God*. Jesus said seek and you will *find*. Period at the end of that sentence. Emphasis here on the word "find." Seeking is not supposed to be a lifelong ordeal. Yes, we are daily *enjoying* Him. Constantly growing in a greater and greater revelation of His fullness. But it's a fullness we already have. In fact, God was never impressed with your seeking to begin with. He was impressed with *His Son* who searched you out. You didn't choose Him; He chose you (John 15:16). You will never be able to boast in your own ability to *choose* the Lord or seek Him out – you can only thank Him.

And Isaiah boldly says, *"**I was found by those who did not seek me**; I revealed myself to those who did not ask for me"* (Rom. 10:20, NIV).

When Christ talks about seeking first His Kingdom, this is not about works or self-effort. The moral of the story is about having your priorities in order. God stuff over worldly stuff. When you got saved, you found the Kingdom He told you to seek.

We make such a virtue out of *seeking*. We think that God is somehow impressed when someone is "hungry" for spirituality. Even if that hunger is completely misguided, we think that it is still somehow noble to be a *seeker*. "Joe does a lot of drugs and meditates to the Dalai Lama everyday. At least he's a *seeker!"* Jews are seeking. Muslims are seeking. Seeking is still human effort. We have a wealth of seeking language. Very little *finding* language in the church.

The New Covenant is a finding covenant. An arrival. An enjoyment of the Promise Land that we have entered.

Isn't your claim to Christianity a very boast that you are no longer looking for answers, but that you have found Him? Christianity is the only religion that can scandalously boast that we are no longer seeking, but have confidently laid hold of God. It seems such an arrogant boast! I have *all* of God! This is the stumbling block of the ages.

Seeking is a pre-Christ action.

One would say, "But doesn't He reward those who earnestly seek Him?" That is Hebrews 11:6. Read the beginning of the verse, "And without *faith* it is impossible to please God." God is impressed with faith. Believe that you are in union by the finished work of the cross.

The Lord once spoke to an anonymous mystic, asking her this, "If I am the air you breathe, if you are in Me and I am in you, why are you looking for Me?" She said, "At once I felt so close to God that I could never describe it. ..." [36]

Hungry or Satisfied?

Another big catch phrase today is "get hungry." You have to *get hungry* for God. How can I do that, when I've been feasting on the Lamb? God doesn't want you to be hungry. He wants you to be *fully satisfied*. The admission of hunger is an admission of lack. A hungry child is a sign of bad parenting. It is an assertion that Christ's sacrifice was not a good enough meal for you.

Do you need something more than His cross? Let the cross be the only thing that mesmerizes you.

I have begun to become a bit of a stickler on language. Most of our worship songs are begging God to do things He has already done. Most songs are singing from an Old Covenant perspective. Some are so chock

---

[36] Fr. Juan Arintero, *The Song of Songs: A Mystical Exposition* (Rockford, IL: Tan Books and Publishers, Inc., 1974, 1992), 403.

full of unbelief and bad theology, they might as well be full of swear words in God's ears. Good for an unbeliever to sing, but ridiculous for a believer to sing.

How many people ask God to "*open the Heavens?*" He already did that. Checked that one right off the prayer list when He died, so you don't need to ask for it anymore. Just believe. The fringier prophets of today now have all sorts of make-believe, Heaven-opening techniques. Because the gospel is neither being preached nor believed, charismatics are turning by the droves to new age.

All sorts of crazy lines fill our songs today:

"Lord prepare me to be a sanctuary ..." *Where do you think He lives right now?*

"Take me into the Holy of Holies ..." *Where do you think you live right now?*

"Lord have mercy, Christ have mercy ..." *Why do you think He died for you?*

"Purify my heart ..." *Didn't He give you a new one?*
I understand that people may benefit from these kinds of songs when they are coming to faith. But now that faith has arrived, let us speak maturely.

But by far, the "*open up the Heavens*" slogan is one of the more popular mottos of unbelief today, accompanied by obligatory groans, pleas and mournful entreaties. It sounds like a romantic request indeed, but it is an accomplished one. Opening and closing the heavens is not an on again, off again affair.

"Last week, when our worship leader hit that one chord on the guitar, *the Heavens opened up!*"

Wow. All we needed was a guitarist I suppose! If Jimi Hendrix had come a little earlier, perhaps Jesus didn't need to die after all? I don't deny that you had a good service and that people *felt* the Glory. But in reality, the Glory of God was already there. You just became aware of it. God's heavenly presence is not a fleeting, or gradually oncoming thing that is subject to the whim of the congregation's mood. In fact, the Bible never even says that His Glory is a future-coming thing. It's already here.

Continuous Open Heavens

Some people think that one day His Glory – His manifest presence – will cover the Earth as the waters cover the seas. That's a misquote of Habakkuk 2:14, which actually says that the "knowledge" of the Glory will one day cover the Earth. Instead, read Isaiah 6:3 which says that Heaven and Earth are *right now* full of His Glory. The Glory is here, but one day the whole Earth will be aware of it! One day everyone will have a knowledge or "God consciousness" that His Spirit is everywhere we go. He's in Wal-Mart. He's in the 7-11. He's at the grocery store. He's at your backslidden husband's cubicle at work. He's all around you as you read this book. Heaven and Earth are full of His Glory.

The whole point of the cross was to open the heavens. The veil of Christ's flesh was torn and all of Heaven was opened with it. If you think you need to do one iota more than to believe in the work of the cross, in order to open the heavens, you are asking for a subjective, emotional roller coaster ride. By constantly believing that Heaven is open, you can constantly experience it.

The problem is that people believe their actions or atmospheric conditions are necessary to open the heavens. That's why they only *feel* or *experience* it occasionally ... whenever the stars align for them. I am no longer dependent on music, an hour of prayer, a good sermon or a fast to feel the presence of God. Those things distract me if I am depending on them. The reason I am constantly experiencing the drunken Glory of His presence – the reason I am constantly aware of the visionary realm and the reality of the angelic – is because I believe the cross opened it all up to me permanently. We must simply trust the message.

You will not live a consistent, daily life of open heavens reality if you can't acknowledge that you are in permaglory. Never depend one iota on your own performance to accomplish what He has already done. Believers are little carriers of open heavens everywhere they go.

Jesus told Nathaniel in John 1 by word of knowledge that he had just seen him sitting under the fig tree. That represented that Nathaniel was under the old Jewish covenant. Amazed at this prophetic word, Nathaniel immediately believed in Jesus. Jesus essentially said, *you believe just because I had a word of knowledge?* He said to Nathaniel, "I tell you the truth, you shall see Heaven open, and the angels of God ascending and descending on the Son of Man" (John 1:50, NIV).

Jesus is saying here that He is not simply a prophet. Don't be mesmerized by visions or words of knowledge. Even a psychic can get those. Jesus is saying *I am more than a prophet*. He said *I am Jacob's Ladder*. That the angels move up and down on Him. Jesus was saying, "I am Open Heavens."

You have Jacob's Ladder living inside you right now! Your belly is an international airport for angels. Open Heavens is a *person*.

Enthroned in Union

As a believer, you are now seated in heavenly places. Which heavenly place? Right on the throne in Him. Right now, whether you realize it or not, you are in the creamy center of Heaven's Twinkie! You are in the gooey sweet middle. You are not in the outer court, washing your hands, trying to gain entrance. You are in the sticky honey pot of the Holy of Holies. Now, you are just passively enjoying your new existence and shining that reality outward to the world.

The disciples James and John got it wrong when they were arguing over who gets the best box seats in Heaven. We all get the best spot – right in Daddy's lap.

And he raised us with Christ, and through our union with Christ Jesus made us sit down with Him in Heaven (Eph. 2:6, GSPD).

... raised us with Him from the dead, and enthroned us with Him in the heavenly realms as being in Christ Jesus (Eph. 2:6, WEY).

Where do you think Heaven is? Out in outer space somewhere, three light years past Alpha Centauri? No. This verse tells us that Heaven is located *in Christ.*

Furthermore, Paul had a revelation that we are *citizens* of Heaven (Phi. 3:20). That is the land of your dwelling. Life is not about getting a higher ranking in Heaven. Rewards and crowns may come, but you must recognize Him as your reward. He is the pearl of great price. He is the Delight of Paradise. All your crowns will be cast at His feet. You are not laboring for something you don't have. Your co-laboring with Christ comes only as a joyful overflow *because* of what you have.

Don't be mesmerized by those who teach heavily on different *levels* of Heaven. They'll use body language and innuendos to assert that they fly first class while you're stuck in economy. Those who give tools for cracking open a "brass heaven" or clearing out principalities in the second heaven have many fanciful strategies and elaborate imaginations. They love to sell you these tools, keys and strategies. But the danger lies in emphasizing what *you* must do to ascend or descend. And that detracts from the message. Speakers love to make boasts that are beyond themselves in order to appear spiritually elite – though on the surface, they may delight in false humility. Heaven may have levels, but I guarantee that you are nestled into the best one! Your efforts are not necessary. Don't try to help God out in a Heaven-opening game. You're a kid with a chemistry set who's liable to blow the thing up.

But the righteousness that is by faith says: "Do not say in your heart, 'Who will ascend into Heaven?'" (that is, to bring Christ down)" or 'Who will descend into the deep?'" (that is, to bring Christ up from the dead) (Rom. 10:6-7, NIV).

Second heavens you may clear out, but I guarantee it will never be from your ascetic observances or rightly articulated declarations. It happens just because you show up! Everywhere you go, the Kingdom is released, expanded and confirmed because you are a born-again son of God. It is simply by *being* who you are and boasting in Christ alone that the Kingdom is manifest.

Part 4 ... THE GALATIAN BEWITCHMENT

Much of the church today is under some degree of the Galatian bewitchment. Paul's letter to the Galatian church is chronologically considered to be the first New Testament book ever written. The issue facing those early believers is likely the first, foremost and central problem ever to surface in the church universal.

O you dear idiots of Galatia, who saw Jesus Christ the crucified so plainly, who has been casting a spell over you? (Gal. 3:1, PHI)

Paul uses a term of affection for the Galatians – literally *beloved idiots*! If he openly declares their idiocy, be sure that he equally spells out his love for them. He asks, *who has bewitched you*? Wasn't Jesus Christ clearly portrayed as crucified among you? Didn't we paint a superbly clear picture of the crucified Christ as your ultimate and only connection to Heaven?

The Galatians had jumped back into formulas and effort to obtain "more" from God. This was a very severe issue. In fact, Paul sat down and wrote his letter to them *by hand*, which was not his usual custom. And he withheld his customary niceties. "Note that in this Epistle alone he plunges straight into his upbraiding; in every other letter he first says such courteous things of his readers as he truthfully can," notes C.T. Wood.[37]

I shall ask you one simple question: Did you receive the Spirit by trying to keep the Law or by believing the message of the gospel? Surely you can't be so idiotic as to think that a man begins his spiri-

---

[37] Wood, *The Life, Letters and Religion of St. Paul*, 75.

125

tual life in the Spirit and then completes it by revert-
ing to outward observances? Has all your painful
experience brought you nowhere? I simply cannot
believe it of you! Does God, who gives you His
Spirit and works miracles among you, do these
things because you have obeyed the Law or be-
cause you have believed the gospel? Ask your-
selves that (Gal. 3:2-5, PHI).

The Galatians lost their fundamental understanding of union with God. They had started in a revelation of Christ's cross, but reverted to formulas and human-effort to further their relationship with Him. It is the same principle that says, "Jesus saved me, now it's up to me to improve my own spirituality." It reduces the cross of Christ to an initiation rite – a kindergarten class that we *move on* from as we mature. While this is a prevalent problem in every stream of the church, it finds its most fertile soil in the charismatic circles.

Not every church is focused on miracles and spirit baptism. For non-charismatic churches, the bewitchment usually manifests in this way: it emphasizes a need to get *my own character* into alignment, *learn* more about God or *serve* Him in order to appease Him. And this form of self-reliance for personal growth is surely indicative of where the Galatians slipped. But in charismatic crowds, the spell flourishes in a different way. Much more in its original version – people feel they must turn to self-effort to get *more* of Holy Spirit or to work better and more fantastic miracles.

A number of charismatics today will even go as far to say we should not preach the cross anymore, because it's just the *basics*. We need to mature and move on to other things. I tell you that whenever the cross is not central and expounded upon, people will jump head-long into the bewitchment of human effort. I know of a number of prophets who give a courtesy nod to the cross, then expound on all their fantastic adventures in seer land. They occasionally use the blood of Jesus fairy wand in their imaginary battles with dragons and principalities. But these guys have missed the boat. Though some of their experiences may be indeed valid, they've unwittingly become disconnected from the head. The person of Jesus is not simply a door into experience, He is the destination.

Charismatic Pharisees

In Paul's day, there were quite a number of preachers who were gifted to work miracles, yet their theology was complete bunk. Often, they would follow in Paul's footsteps, trying to draw new believers back into an observance of rules and regulations. They are very subtle. Masters at what they do. Some of the most popular men on the stage. They come bearing stories of elaborate supernatural happenings too. You have to remember that even the Pharisees were charismatic – there were Pharisee exorcists; they believed in angels; they believed in a final resurrection. The Sadducees didn't believe in much of the supernatural, but the Pharisees did. Belief in the supernatural alone does not protect you from religiosity. Belief in the supernatural, without a foundation of grace, will just make you superstitious. Charismatics make the best Pharisees.

As Charismatics, our appreciation for the supernatural is never problematic. The problem is that we don't appreciate the supernatural enough. We should be so utterly dependent on the miraculous in our daily lives that we see every breath as a sign and wonder. The immensity of it all should make us give up trying to affect it all on our own. We give up and trust.

Self-effort, or *law mentality*, is the issue at hand. The emphasis on self to achieve miracles, spiritual empowerment or higher revelation is the Galatian bewitchment. It's not a problem of cessationism. The bewitchment allows you to embrace miracles, prophetic revelation, etc. – as long as it pulls you away from the simplicity of the cross to get it.

Eastern and Western Minds

Your deepest wisdom ... the most mysterious secret ever revealed to mankind has been plainly published.

Want to know the secrets of the universe? It is Jesus. He is the *"that mystic secret of God, [which is] Christ (the Anointed One)"* (Col. 2:2, AMP). Holy Spirit always points us to the Lamb that was slain.

The simplicity of Christ crucified was a major offense to the Jewish mentality. The Jewish mentality of that day was synonymous with all of eastern culture. Eastern cultures are motivated and impressed with miracles, signs and wonders. The eastern mindset is generally open to the supernatural. Visit Africa, Asia and the Middle Eastern world. They have no problem believing in a spirit realm. In an Arabic country, if someone has a dream, people will take time out of their daily routine just to listen. The spirit realm is not taken lightly.

The Jews, therefore, wanted their Messiah to come with light shows, parting Red Seas and opening up a can of Rambo on their Roman oppressors. It was a scandal to think that all their answers were found in the broken body of a man who died a criminal's death. Moreover, they were offended that all the supernatural *power and Glory of God* – which they had strived so diligently to legally access – was being given as a *free gift*. This was scandalous.

THE GALATIAN BEWITCHMENT

On the other hand, let us not forget a different clientele of folks who lived in the *western world*. The Jews were not the only ones balking at the gospel. Paul's message was an equal opportunity offender!

The western world was represented by the *Greek* mindset of the day. Rationalistic, reason-based, intellect oriented. Greeks were not moved by miracles, but rather by philosophy. And many did not want to give Paul the time of day. The gospel just seemed absurd and ridiculous hogwash. The Greco-rationalistic mind is more impressed with profound teaching and scholarship. The Greek mind is found throughout the western world today – America, Europe, Australia, etc. We want teachings, philosophies, more articulate sermons. Not only was the Greek offended by Paul's simple message, but probably also by the ecstatic, childlike way he preached it. This was a message that was more *caught than taught*. It was too simple, too easy, too emotional for the Greek.

But we do not allow the Jew to trust in miracles, nor the Greek to trust in intellect.

When in the wisdom of God the world was allowed to fail in its effort to comprehend Him by the use of its own wisdom, He arranged for the salvation of believers through the "stupidity" of plain and simple preaching.

So while the Jews ask for a sign and the Greeks look for a philosophy, we preach Christ crucified, a stumbling-block to the Jews and stupidity to the Greeks, but to the elect Christ the power of God and the wisdom of God. God's "stupid cross" reveals a greater wisdom than that of men, and His weakness a greater strength than theirs (1 Cor. 1:24-25, WAND).

We see both of these same dueling mentalities in the church today. Some denominations want more "wisdom" (i.e. seminary degrees, intellectual theology, more four-point messages, turning church into a mere "classroom" of learning and theorizing). That's western.

Other denominations are impressed with the charismatic sham-wow element of "look at the miracles I can perform!" That's Eastern.

To the intellectual, the cross is stupid. Of no more significance than the latest guy executed in Texas. But to the charismatic, it is a *scandal* or "scandalon" because it discredits everything we've ever done to become more *spiritual*.

Again, let me clarify – we embrace both the miraculous and sound theology. Paul was a brilliant, master theologian. If you have made it this far through the book, you appreciate theology as well. Paul was a fantastic miracle worker – even inanimate cloths that were touched to his body healed the sick and drove out demons. We should never oppose theology or the miraculous. We value both. We should never choose Word or Spirit over one another. But the Main Thing is always the Main Thing – *the broken body of Christ.* He is our ultimate Wisdom and Power.

The Hebraic and Greek worldviews are both reconciled in Christ.

Wide Open Access

For starters, let me say that we are living in amazing days as God is restoring a supernatural, Kingdom perspective to the church. We have always and will always be staunch proponents for a thoroughly miraculous, experiential Christianity. It is incredible that people are corporately realizing that healing, creative miracles, mystical powers and all manner of bizarre wonders are part of our inheritance for today. But we do not *work* for that inheritance. My children do not work for their inheritance, I do.

People are getting enthusiastic about the supernatural these days. This is a refreshing change from the dull, powerless, naturalistic Christianity of days gone by. There is no limit to the nature or quality of the miraculous God wants to pour out. But the first moment we attempt to climb into Kingdom miracles or to somehow access the heavens, we have surely missed the plot altogether – and as Paul says, we have been "alienated from Christ; you have fallen away from grace" (Gal. 5:4, NIV).

Understand that this is subtle, but vitally important to grasp. I have learned this the hard way. But I have also listened to many of the most popular prophets on the "prophetic circuit" today. I am friends with many of them. I can vouch safe in saying – in utmost humility – that most of them attribute some form of self-effort to their gifting. It's a sad state of bewitchment.

Observance of any law – whether Levitical law or a general moral code – never purchases union for you. Nor can you do one lick of extra curricular courses to get "more" of Holy Spirit than what you already have. The problem is, you just don't know what you have.

In the same way, techniques and formulas for "opening the heavens" or "accessing the Glory realm" put the emphasis on you and your disciplines – diminishing the person of Christ. Believe that you already have a Heaven open so wide it cannot be stretched further. The opening is as big as God. Because God is the one who was opened. Charles Spurgeon says the following:

This is no narrow pipe through which a thread-like stream may wind its way, it is a channel of amazing depth and breadth, along whose breadth and length a ponderous volume of living water may roll its strength. Behold He hath set before us an open door. ... This city of communion hath many pearly gates, every several gate is of one pearl, and each gate is thrown open to the uttermost that we may enter, assured of welcome. If there were but one small loophole through which to talk with Jesus, it would be a high privilege to thrust a word of fellowship through the narrow door; how much we are blessed in having so large an entrance![38]

Earlier, I mentioned one of the top questions our ministry regularly receives: *How do I get drunk in the Spirit?*

Well, for starters, you should stop trying! If you are *trying* to have a spiritual experience, the Bible has a word for that: *divination*. All self-effort toward ascension is firmly frowned upon by God. I am not trying to have a spiritual experience. *I believe I am already having one.*

I believe I am already in the House of Wine, thanks to Christ's work. I rely on His efforts, not my own. If I don't feel anything, that's irrelevant. When I relax and trust that I'm already fully tanked, I begin to enjoy the drink. Feeling follows faith. His work is the substance and source from which I am drinking.

Effortless Infilling

Let's put the "drunk in the Spirit" analogy aside for a moment. Perhaps that terminology seems foreign to

---

[38] Charles Spurgeon, "Bands of Love or Union to Christ." (*Sword and Trowel*, Sept. 1865).

you. Instead, think merely of being "filled" with the Spirit or moving in the miraculous. How many people struggle, strive and do all sorts of mental and emotional gyrations in an attempt to encounter Holy Spirit?

We have separated our Calvary from our Pentecost. It is not your waiting, soaking, lingering or your tarrying that gives you Holy Spirit. He was poured out to you through the broken body of Jesus. Your prayers, fasting and strictest ascetic disciplines do not add one more drop of God to your life than what you've already received in Christ.

We have shown how it is erroneous to sanctify ourselves. But religion also appeals equally to human effort for climbing into mystical experiences. Again – mystical experiences are valid and encouraged. Climbing into them is not. Peter and Paul never climbed into trances or visionary encounters. In Acts 10 and 22, we see that both apostles "fell" into their trances. Get this picture in your mind of effortlessly sinking into Christ.

Let me say it again. Your attempts to get closer to God are the very things that alienate you from grace. The attempt itself negates the fact that you are already 100 percent connected to Him.

What is Religion?

Although it's late in the game for such a basic topic, I think I need to back track a few paces and give you a simple definition of *religion*. Again, I will borrow from Robert Capon:

Religion is the attempt on the part of human beings to establish a right relationship between themselves

*and something outside themselves – something
they think to be of life-shaping importance.*[39]

This holistic definition applies just as much to Bud-
dhism and yoga as it does jogging or dieting. Whether
we're trying to reconcile ourselves to a better physique,
mother earth or Allah – that much is irrelevant. Religion
is religion. The whole clockwork depends on *you getting things right.* The end result – happiness, nirvana,
enlightenment, whatever – is *up to you.*

There's just one problem. *It doesn't work.*

This is where Paul rejoiced. He'd been given a "get out
the religion business for free" ticket at the cross. This
master religionist was utterly delivered from his *God-
pleasing.* Every attempt at setting his own record
straight with the Man Upstairs was shown for what it
was – a scrappy parallel universe of dogmas and good-
for-nothing jumping jacks that had nothing to do with
reality and didn't bring him an inch closer to home.

*What actually took place is this: I tried keeping
rules and working my head off to please God, and it
didn't work. So I quit being a "law man" so that I
could be God's man* (Gal. 2:19, MSG).

Capon continues to unfold for us the concept that
Christianity is *no religion.*

*In spite of the fact that the Good News of Jesus
Christ ... has been seen as a religion by outsiders
and been sold as one by its adherents, it is not a*

---

[39] Capon, *Health, Money & Love and Why We Don't Enjoy Them,*
27.

*religion at all. Rather, it is the announcement of **the end of religion.**[40]*

Charismatic Voodoo

I don't know what fish bowls you swim in, Christian or non-Christian, Methodist or Baptist. But I guarantee you've met a few bottom feeders in your tank that are obsessed with the stagnant rot of religion.

For myself (and quite a number of my readers), we would ordinarily be lumped together with the *charismatic stream* of the church. That's our little fishbowl. Most of the guppies in here think it's the whole ocean, but it's not. We're just on one tiny shelf of the pet store, and most kids laugh at us when they walk by. Nevertheless, it's *my stream*. I'm familiar with it. I'm not jumping ship. If I were a fish bowl cleaner, I would be best suited to scrub and shock treat the religion out of a charismatic bowl than any other.

But I will say this. For all their loud yapping against the evils of "religion," the prophetic/charismatic church is dumbstruck and blinded by the Galatian bewitchment.

There is lots of charismatic voodoo going on in the church today. We love the creative, colorful, wacky way that prophetic people express themselves in worship. But never let the expression become a crutch or an initiation rite. On a minor level, you see the guy who gets a little too absorbed with prophetic acts – he has to blow his shofar a certain way or pour his anointing oil on seven mountains in order to get a spiritual breakthrough. And there are deeper levels of fringe – people

---

[40] Capon, *Health, Money & Love and Why We Don't Enjoy Them*, 31.

who eat gold powder for heightened supernatural experiences, return to kosher diets, etc.

But those are extremes – not the primary modes by which people get bewitched. The spell is much more subtle on the majority of folks. It is usually through the "mundane" disciplines that people get caught up in this – *prayer, fasting, etc.* Disciplines which seem innocent enough, but which quickly become the subconscious indicators of how we gauge our own spirituality. In other words, we appeal to our own *spiritual activity* rather than the finished work of Christ to define our identity. This was the problem of the ones in Matthew 7 who approached Christ on the basis of their prophetic and deliverance activity.

Not everyone who says to me, "Lord, Lord," will enter the Kingdom of Heaven, but only he who does the will of My Father who is in Heaven. Many will say to Me on that day, "Lord, Lord, did we not prophesy in Your name, and in Your name drive out demons and perform many miracles?" Then I will tell them plainly, "I never knew you. Away from Me, you evildoers!" (Matt. 7:21-23, NIV)

Jesus was in no way condemning prophecy or deliverance here! The problem was that these men pointed to their *own works* – albeit lofty ones – as their justification for accessing Heaven. Even your best works are considered evil by God if they are your claim to justification. How do we do the "will of My Father who is in Heaven" and thereby gain entrance to the Kingdom?

Jesus answered, "The work of God is this: to believe in the one he has sent" (John 6:29, NIV).

Even this faith is a gift! Generally, charismatics and mainliners alike would not point to prayer, fasting and other disciplines in a salvific sense. But in a practical sense, they think these things bring them closer into union with God. And this implies a deficiency on Christ's part to achieve a full and complete union.

The Gospel Changes Everything

If our efforts are not necessary for salvation, union or acceptance with God, how then do we now view prayer, fasting, worship, giving and other spiritual disciplines?

Everything must now be seen through the lens of what Christ has accomplished. You are no longer climbing into something; rather it is spilling out of you.

Let's look first at prayer. People think that by praying, they are drawing closer to God. Instead, it is because you are already in union with God that you get to enjoy prayer.

People make a work of prayer, pointing to Paul's exhortation to "pray continually" (1 Thess. 5:17). Paul did not mean to shout at the wall in tongues and pray for the president twenty-four hours a day. Some take this so literally and legalistically they're afraid of losing points if not jabbering a full twenty-four hours instead of 23.5 hours in the prayer room. Twenty-four hour prayer is a trendy thing today, but be careful of religion in a shiny new package.

By praying continually, Paul was not just referring to verbal prayer. Even Jesus tells us not to pray for the same thing over and over, blabbering away like the hypocrites and the pagans do (Matt. 6:5-7). The only way to truly pray continually is to *practice the presence of God*. It is about a relationship/heart issue, not an external exercise of articulation and sweat. The practice

THE GALATIAN BEWITCHMENT

of His presence is simply the effortless, loving aware-
ness of Him at all times. It is about enjoying the person
of Christ, which you already have. Consider what
Brother Lawrence writes:

> *I have quitted all forms of devotion and set prayers*
> *but those to which my state obliges me. And I make*
> *it my business only to persevere in His holy pres-*
> *ence, wherein I keep myself by a simple attention,*
> *and a general fond regard to God ... which often*
> *causes me joys and raptures inwardly, and some-*
> *times also outwardly, so great, that I am forced to*
> *use means to moderate them, and prevent their*
> *appearance to others. ...*
>
> *At other times, when I apply myself to prayer, I feel*
> *all my spirit and all my soul lift itself up without any*
> *care or effort of mine, and it continues as it were*
> *suspended and firmly fixed in GOD, as in its centre*
> *and place of rest.*[41]

The great saint Brother Lawrence – known as a man of
continual prayer – says he *stopped* praying! He started
enjoying, and just rolling with the Glory – wherever his
"state" obliged him. He just followed the joys of God's
prompting, wherever he felt the cloud leading him.

True Prayer

If I am standing in line at Burger King, ordering a happy
meal while blissed out in the presence of God – then I
am in prayer. And I may even be fasting! Whenever
you are enjoying your harmony with His presence, this
is prayer. Verbal intercession is just one type of prayer.

---

[41] Brother Lawrence, *The Practice of the Presence of God: The
Best Rule of a Holy Life* (New York: Fleming H. Revell Co., 1895),
25-26.

138

Consider tongues, for instance, where Paul says, "Rapt in the Spirit, he is uttering mystic secrets" (1 Cor. 14:2, WAY). The highest forms of prayer – worship, ecstasy – are always passive states of the heart toward God.

It is funny that so many people think they are helping God out with their prayers. Did you know that prayer was originally something designed to help *you* out?

Hey God, I can't do this on my own! Help!

Prayer doesn't do God any favors. It's a way to acknowledge that *He* gives the favors. Whenever you think you are helping God out, you claim to be His benefactor, and Him the needy beneficiary.

Prayer, much like the Sabbath, was a gift to assist you. Jesus said, "The Sabbath was made for man, not man for the Sabbath" (Mark 2:27). By encouraging prayer, Paul was not advocating human effort. He was advocating dependence.

Never let someone put a yoke of bondage on you. It was for freedom that Christ set you free.

What About Fervent Prayer?

It is thought that prayer is most effective when it is *strenuous*. God is not impressed with grit. He's impressed with faith. Such people often point to James, who said, "The effectual *fervent* prayer of a righteous man availeth much" (Jas. 5:17, KJV). Taking this word "fervent" or "earnest," slave masters have heaped all sorts of pressure on believers over the years – trying to get them to push and strain and pop a blood vessel in the prayer closet. I once heard a famous teacher say, "A preacher is not worth a plug nickel in the pulpit if he doesn't pray for two hours a day!" If I were counting on my own prayers to make me worthy, what a putrid preacher I would be!

A number of translators see through the guise. They rightly recognize that James is not saying to pray strenuously. Rather, the *prayer itself* is powerful if you are a righteous man. And you are the righteousness of God in Christ Jesus. This word "fervent" is *energo*.[42] It means a prayer that *works*. It performs. It gets the job done. He does not suggest that the nature of your prayer has to be striving. No need to pop a hernia over this. This is where we get our word "energy." Prayers that are effortless, trusting ones – reliant upon God by faith – are the ones infused with God's energy.

... The prayer of a righteous person has great power as it is working (Jas. 5:17, ESV).

God wants faith – *restful trust or belief* – not human effort. Furthermore, if we don't learn to play, we'll never really know how to pray.

One question we often receive about spiritual disciplines is this: *But don't people see results from diligent prayer and fasting?*

Results happen, yes. But *faith* – not the *prayers themselves* – brought the answer. Often, people are diligently banging their head against the wall in the prayer room – or undergoing a fast – when along the way, faith slips in and knocks them upside the head. That faith releases a breakthrough in their lives. But here's the problem. Rather than attributing the breakthrough to *faith*, they quickly attribute the victory to the *discipline* they were exercising at the time. Self takes credit.

---

[42] Strong, *Exhaustive Concordance of the Bible*, Entry 1754.

140

Don't be Mesmerized

People often think they are preaching *deeper truths* just because their subject matter involves prophetic paradigms or the supernatural. Yet their teachings are laced with keys and techniques that are formulaic. What indicates you are really teaching a deeper truth? *You affirm the simplicity of Christ.*

Paul said that the Galatians were bamboozled. They had been hoodwinked, just as the serpent tricked Eve away from the simplicity of devotion to Christ. The desire for the prophetic, healing or even more fantastic miracles is perfectly wonderful. What's not wonderful is the pressure of taking matters into your own hands to get there.

The Galatian bewitchment, very simply, means to *work for the gift.* It is the attempt to get something you already have.

Charismatic speakers love to give you a list of keys how to get the anointing that's on their life. What they rarely tell you is that they received it as a *gift.* That line of reasoning doesn't sell very well on the book table.

The worst and most mesmerizing of the bunch are the ones that pressure you into all manner of strenuous, ascetic disciplines. One of the trendiest pop disciplines of today is that of *fasting.* There are some out there who boast in the dozens upon dozens of forty-day fasts. These guys never fail to mesmerize the crowds with their self-abasement. Though they wouldn't say it, they take great delight in making you feel lazy, less spiritual and incompetent in comparison to them.

I have determined to be mesmerized by nothing but the cross. As Paul stated, "I resolved to know *nothing* while

I was with you except Jesus Christ and Him crucified" (1 Cor. 2:2, NIV).

A Chosen Fast

Fasting is one of the most grueling outward obser-vances, and for some reason, religious folks just think pain equals gain. They think it will make you more like Christ and change the world. Although it is promoted on some of the fanciest web sites and largest confer-ences today, fasting is two clicks shy of outright gnosti-cism for a New Testament believer.

Fasting does not draw you closer to God.

There is not a single New Testament mandate to fast. But you would think it was on every page of the Bible thanks to the propagating efforts of its practitioners.

The closest scripture one can find is Matthew 17:21 – still in the pre-crucifixion era – where Jesus supposedly says that some demons come out only through "prayer and fasting." Upon closer look, scholars realized that the oldest manuscripts do not even include the word "fasting" in this passage, nor does Jesus use it in the other synoptic gospel account of this same conversa-tion (Mark 9:29). For this reason, the *New International Version*, *English Standard Version*, *English Revised Version* and *New Living Translation* – among others – do not even include that verse.

Whether or not the verse is legitimate really is not the issue, nor should we question the infallibility of the Word. We are not opposed to fasting. But true fasting needs to be properly *defined*. Even in the Old Cove-nant, the Lord spoke of a *better* fast that had nothing to do with food abstinence. It has to do with issues of the heart and *sharing* your food with the poor (Isa. 58).

Fasting is a heart issue.

I fast all the time! I fast *depression, demons, evil, frowns, sin, poverty, sickness* and *religion* just to name a few things. Did you know that every single one of these is a billion times better than a food fast? I do not exaggerate at all. God doesn't care about your McDonalds. He cares about your heart.[1]

If you are fasting food, but not feasting on Him, you are wasting your time. In this sense, we live a fasted life-style, because abstaining from inward sin is not an oc-casional thing. It's normative Christianity.[1]

Keep the Feast

Unlike muslims or gnostic sects, which vilify the human body itself, the Lord never allowed the Jewish people to be overly harsh on their bodies with fasting. There was only one required fast of the year. It was the Day of Atonement. The day was fulfilled when the Lamb of God was slain to atone for the sins of the world. Now, that day has been turned into the biggest feast of all!

The same was true for Esther. She fasted on the verge of national genocide. But now that day – Purim – has also been turned into a day of wine drinking and cele-bration for Jews! The potential holocaust turned into a holiday. Feasts far outnumber fasts in the Old Testa-ment culture.

We are now only directed to *keep the feast* (1 Cor. 5:8). We are feasting on the Lamb that was slain, who is continually before us.

See how the Pharisees came along whining about this:

Their next complaint was that Jesus' disciples were feasting instead of fasting. "John the Baptist's disciples are constantly going without food, and praying," they declared, "and so do the disciples of the Pharisees. Why are yours wining and dining?" (Luke 5:33, TLB).

He said it was impossible for His disciples to fast because the Bridegroom was with them.

Jesus answered, "How can the guests of the Bridegroom fast while He is with them? They cannot, so long as they have Him with them. But the time will come when the Bridegroom will be taken from them, and on that day they will fast" (Mark 2:19-20, NIV).

Do you know how long "that day" lasted? It was the day when He was killed. Could you eat if your friend died? Now the Bridegroom is closer to you than He was with Peter, James and John. He lives *inside* of you.

Commentator Adam Clarke points out that the early church only kept one fast per year, which was a predecessor to modern day Lent.

"This fast is pretended to be kept by many, in the present day, in commemoration of our Lord's *forty* days' fast in the wilderness; but it does not appear that, in the purest ages of the *primitive Church*, genuine Christians ever pretended that their ... fast was kept for the above purpose. Their fast was kept merely to commemorate the *time* during which Jesus Christ lay under the power of death, which was about forty hours," writes Clarke, adding that over the years, this forty-hour fast grew into something more obnoxious. "They put days in the place of hours; and this absurdity continues in some Christian Churches to the present day."[43]

Abstain from food if you need to diet, or you're trying to clear your head to get some revelation about something. But don't think you're adding virtue to yourself – that's the bewitchment. I have also seen young people fast as a spiritualized excuse to save money. A type of glorified scrimping. Share your food with the poor, but don't blame God for poverty in your life! Clarke is sharp on this point saying, "He who saves a day's expense by a fast, commits an abomination before the Lord."

Jesus' emphasis on fasting was not to forbid it, but one could easily argue that He downplayed it. If you're going to fast, then cheer up at least and don't be dismal! "Jesus asked, 'Do happy men fast?" (Luke 5:34, TLB). Don't miss the whole point, which is joy unspeakable and full of Glory. Surely don't wreck everyone else's party so that they feel sorry for you.

When you practice some appetite-denying discipline to better concentrate on God, don't make a production out of it. It might turn you into a small-time celebrity but it won't make you a saint (Matt. 6:16, MSG).

If you know of any particular minister's fasting routines, don't be impressed. The fact he told you about them just disqualified him from the benefit.

When you fast don't be like the hypocrites who go out all depressed. Their glum self-denial they hope you will applaud. Truthfully, they already have their

---

[43] Clarke, *Commentary on the Whole Bible*, Excerpt from Matt. 9.

reward. But when you are fasting keep it secret for the Lord ... (Matt. 6:14-16, ECK).

The rare times that fasting is employed by the apostles, it was only to help clear their heads so they could focus to make a big governmental decision, like appointing elders or leaders. For directional purposes only. And even then it didn't always work. In the case of appointing Matthias, they eventually gave up and rolled a dice. For sure, they never did it to twist God's arm to end abortion or to purgate their own souls.

If you enjoy fasting, please continue to do it! If you enjoy it, go for it! But why not have a *supernatural* fast? Many mystics of the church went literally years without eating food. Catherine of Siena fasted eight years straight. Teresa Neuman, who just died in the 1960s, went more than 30 years without food *and water.* And she was even a bit plump! Physicians and church authorities clinically watched her continuously to make sure she wasn't sneaking Oreos under her pillow.

What's the catch? Teresa never forced herself to fast. She enjoyed it. If she even smelled food pass by her doorway, she would dry heave. She didn't want to eat. There was no self-effort involved in her fasting.

There is nothing wrong with fasting unless you are *forcing yourself* to give something to the Lord. The flavor of religion is always forcing oneself to do something.

Religion is Forced

Remember the story when Samuel was supposed to make a sacrifice for the Israelites before they went out to battle in 1 Samuel 13? King Saul started getting nervous when Samuel appeared to be late. He was scared spitless of the Philistines, who outnumbered him like the sands on the seashore. Saul took matters into his own hands and made the sacrifice himself. He should have waited for Samuel – a type of Christ – to make it for him.

Samuel then shows up. And what does Saul say? *I forced myself and offered the burnt offering* (1 Sam. 13:12, NASB).

Religion is compelling yourself to do what only Jesus could do for you. A number of ministries today focus on getting young people pumped up about fasting. Young people are passionate and looking for a purpose to rally around. It's a shame that they are hyped and exploited into dead works. But many will awake to grace in the coming days to be powerful grace preachers.

The Solid Fact is Christ

The Galatians were not the only early believers to get caught up into "do-this-do-that" religion after they first heard the gospel. This seemed to be a common problem across the board. In Heaven, we will never stink the place up with our own do-do! We will only boast in what He has done. The Colossian church fell under a similar mesmerization – the concept that outward forms and observances heightened their spirituality. Paul had to address the Colossian bewitchment as well:

> *In view of these tremendous facts* (that you shared in Christ's death and life), *don't let anyone worry you by criticizing what you eat or drink, or what holy days you ought to observe, or bothering you over new moons or Sabbaths. All these things have at most only a symbolical value; the solid fact is Christ* (Col. 2:16-17, PHI notes mine).

THE GALATIAN BEWITCHMENT

147

Maybe we don't fuss about new moons anymore, but you can fill in the blank here. Whatever is the trendiest spiritual exercise of the day, it is of no value. Everyone has a list of "do this" or "do that" to become prophetic or attain a higher spirituality. Looking to food regulations as a form of spirituality did not end in Paul's day! How trendy and popular is it today to elevate fasting or healthy diet restrictions to a place it never belonged in the New Covenant? Jesus clearly delineated a change of spiritual eras – from one based on outward physical observances, to one based on internal transformation. Don't be intimidated by the crowd who insists you beat down your natural body as a way to gain spiritual benefit. At the end of the day, that is plain old gnosticism. Paul continues speaking to the bewitched Colossians:

Nor let any man cheat you of your joy in Christ by persuading you to make yourselves "humble" and fall down and worship angels (Col. 2:18, PHI).

Surely no one would do that – *steal my joy in Christ* – especially not another Christian? Ha! You'd better believe it! Religion wrecks your party. Steals the sweetness of grace from your life.

As a side note, this passage is not really about the dangers of angel worship. It's about bad charismatic speakers. The spiritual hotshots who like to appear more supernatural than you and sell you formulas. Paul goes on:

Such a man, inflated by an unspiritual imagination, is pushing his way into matters he knows nothing about, and in his cleverness forgetting the head. It is from the head alone that the body, by natural channels, is nourished and built up and grows according to God's laws of growth.

*So if, through your faith in Christ, you are dead to the principles of this world's life, why, as if you were still part and parcel of this world-wide system, do you take the slightest notice of these purely human prohibitions – "Don't touch this," "Don't taste that" and "Don't handle the other?" "This," "that" and "the other" will all pass away after use! I know that these regulations **look wise** with their **self-inspired efforts** at worship, their **policy of self-humbling**, and their **studied neglect of the body**. But in actual practice **they do honour, not to God, but to man's own pride** (Col. 2:18-23, PHI).*

Don't be bamboozled. Don't be hoodwinked. Don't be impressed by what the King James Version calls "will worship." Human determination can accomplish lots of things. Rigorous fasts. Great sacrifice. Couple that together with an extraordinary imagination and a few misplaced scriptures, and what do you have? An intimidating charismatic Pharisee!

In Paul's day, there seemed to be a whole circuit of these will-power guys. And people fed right into a name game. The "who's who" became the talk of the church, and people were distracted from the reality of their easy and complete union with Christ.

I don't want to hear any of you bragging about yourself or anyone else. Everything is already yours as a gift—Paul, Apollos, Peter, the world, life, death, the present, the future—all of it is yours, and you are privileged to be in union with Christ, who is in union with God (1 Cor. 3:21-23, MSG).

We know that the whole aim of the law was to show us how pointless it is to try to live up to it. But when someone rolls into town with legal expertise, fancy formulas and tricks up their sleeve, the best of the best can be lured away from the simplicity of Christ. The law is designed to show you how powerless you are to keep it. One of my favorite passages showing the futility of living up to the law is where Jesus says, "If your eye causes you to sin, pluck it out! ... If your hand causes you to sin, chop it off" (Matt. 5:29-30). It gets no more futile than that. *Want to clean yourselves up? OK. Dismember yourselves!* Jesus was employing irony and outright humor to show us how impossible it is to remove your own sin.

Bewitchers don't bring a frontal assault. They never overtly replace grace with works. They offer simple *additions* to grace. Remember, grace has to be drunk straight. The law is an *add-on.*

Always remember this simple equation: *grace plus law equals law.*

In Paul's day, a minor add-on to the gospel was this: *you need to have your physical body circumcised.* This was such a distraction to Paul's message, he said, "As for those agitators, I wish they would go the whole way and emasculate themselves!" (Gal. 5:12, NIV)

Just to add one thing to Jesus' death – one minor thing like the removal of foreskin – throws you right out of the realm of grace. You are not allowed to lift the slightest finger to affect your own holiness.

You can't have it both ways. Either Jesus perfects, sustains and completes you – or else you have to do the whole thing on your own. Paul said, "Again I declare to every man who lets himself be circumcised that he is obligated to obey the whole law" (Gal. 5:3).

For this reason, we should cringe and shudder with disgust when someone says, "Yes, Jesus' work was

150

enough. But we still need to *position* ourselves. But we still need to *appropriate* it." Anytime you hear someone say the word "but" after mentioning Christ's cross, the next words from their mouth will always be a fairy tale.

What About Discipline?

I should quickly mention that the other disciplines and sacraments of the church are entirely graces for our *benefit*. Not means of helping God out, purifying ourselves or adding to the union we have in Him. Disciplines such as prayer, communion, etc. are modes of enjoying God, not methods of appeasing Him.

Communion is often seen as a depressing, introspective thing where we essentially "clean up" our hearts before we eat the body and blood. What a twisted concept! We have gotten it completely backwards. You don't clean yourself for the table – it is *the table* that cleans you up. If you insist on checking your heart, be sure to check all the depression out of there for the big party! The table of the Lord was a glorious *love feast* for the early church – it was part party, part mystical meal. What Paul says to remove from your heart is any *anxiety*. This is a place of acceptance and trust.

Worship is another discipline that gets mixed up. John Piper often says there is no such thing as disinterested worship or unhappy praise. We have words for people who are into that – we call them *hypocrites*. The point of worship is not clocking in on the job for some obligatory ritual. The essence of worship is *enjoyment*. By definition, worship is a thorough delight – even an addiction if you will – in the object you are worshipping. The gospel removes the motive of obligation from worship, replacing it with the motive of pleasure.

Giving is another discipline that merits mention. Giving doesn't break the curse of poverty – Jesus' broken body did. He bore the thorns and thistles on His sweaty brow, so that you don't have to toil in the thorns and thistles by the sweat of your brow. Does this mean we don't have to give a tithe as they did in the Old Testament? In the New Covenant, God didn't bring us from generous to stingy. Now, we are free to give much more extravagantly, in total abandonment, with no fear of lack. Try giving ninety percent instead of ten and see how it feels. I am a firm believer in sowing and reaping. But before the cross, that principle always worked against my legal, stingy heart. Now that I am a new creation, sowing always works in my favor, because my new heart loves to cheerfully give. I am not free to be stingy, but free to give and move into abundance. I understand now that I am never really giving anything to God. He even gave me the seed that I sow as a gift. Every time I sow it back to Him, it expresses my trust and belief in Him – allowing me to experience real, supernatural multiplication. I no longer do it out of fear of the curse, but out of joy of the reward.

Exercising spiritual gifts is seen by many as an important discipline. But spiritual gifts should be fun. We need to return to child-like innocence with them. I probably speak in tongues more than most people. But rarely am I coherently thinking about it. By no means do I have a legalistic four-hour tongue regiment every day. Nor do I put pressure on others to do that. I love prophecy, and am listening to the Lord all day. But I don't feel a pressure to prophesy over every individual in the shopping mall. Maybe you enjoy that – *go for it!* But never think that the world hinges on your shoulders because you didn't read everyone's mail in Abercrombie. Or consider gifts of healing – some ministers are under such a performance yoke with this. They make the gift of healing their "shtick" and feel it is necessary to demonstrate God's power in that particular way every single time they minister. What if God ever chose to do something else? They wouldn't even know it.

Evangelism is yet another discipline – or perhaps we should say *mandate*. Lots of people get beat up with works-oriented Great Commission sermons. But Matthew 13:39 tells me that I'm not even a harvester – the *angels* are! I can throw my net out all night long, but unless the Lord brings the fish, I am wasting time. I have led well over 100,000 souls to the Lord at this stage of my life. By next year, I expect that number to double or triple. But I find it to be most easy when I ignore the duty or pressure of it. I rarely give a thought to evangelism. I just stay focused on the presence of God, and it happens as an easy byproduct. I don't say that we should be *unaware* of the task at hand or not actively participate. But God opens the doors and quickens me when to walk through them. It is actually Him working through me, and so it's fun and easy. In Acts 2, it was the outpouring of the wine – His glorious presence – that brought in the 3,000-soul harvest on Pentecost. We've wanted the results, but bypassed the person. God is not looking for workers. He's looking for lovers. And the lovers are going to out-work the workers in these days. Radical lovers are going to see an overflow of harvest Glory, and it is going to be completely effortless. You'll just show up, overflowing with His Spirit, and the angels will make stuff happen!

As in all of these disciplines, there's one key ingredient that helps keep the religion out – *fun.* Religion, by nature, demands your serious attention. It is the anti-play. Capon writes:

> *For while it is a truism that nothing that is fun can be done without some measure of discipline, it is practically an eternal truth that nothing that calls for*

discipline will be kept at very long (or very well) if it is not fun.[44]

Sola Fide

Until now, we've spoken much on the true doctrine of *sola fide* – by faith alone. Faith is your access to the Glory realm. Faith is the bond of your mystical union.

What is faith? It means to *believe* or *trust*.

Have you ever wondered what your primary job description is as a Christian? We have spoken quite a bit about dead works so far. So I should repeat again to you what the *real* work is that God requires:

> *Jesus told them, "This is the **only** work God wants from you: **Believe** in the one He has sent"* (John 6:29, NLT).

Frustrated at prophetic teacher Georgian Banov's constant insistence on the finished works of Christ, a pastor once angrily approached him and asked, "What do you expect us to do? Just sit around and *believe*?"

Well, actually you can't even do that! The craziest thing about the gospel is this: *It is impossible to believe.*

The gospel is simply too good to be true. If the message you've heard is not too good to be true, then it probably isn't. The gospel is too easy. Too marvelous. Too extraordinary. Too scandalously good to be true.

And so, even this work is impossible for you to conjure up on your own.

---

[44] Capon, *Health, Money & Love and Why We Don't Enjoy Them*, 144-145.

You can't *make yourself* believe the gospel. It is impossible for you to pump up faith. You can't generate it. No matter how loud you shout, how long you fast or how fervently you exclaim, "I believe!" You still can't work up an ounce of faith.

Faith comes in only one way ... *by grace.*

It is an absolute gift of God that you are able to believe. Amazing grace.

People who have a background in the "Word of Faith" movement that has flourished the last half a century truly have something to be thankful for. We need more and more revelation on faith. However, we never want to slip into the strife that befell some of the folks in that movement. Lots of people end up struggling to work up faith – internally straining to *try, try, try* and believe! Faith becomes an elusive goal that people push and push to achieve.

Faith cannot be conjured up by human willpower. A lot of what people call "faith" is really just their own inflexible determination. By your own worry, willing and contending you cannot add a hair to your head or a day to your life.

Faith is more than a substance. *Faith is a person.* His name is Mr. Faith! Jesus is Faith.

I speak freedom to you right now to be at ease. Sink into trust.

How Do I Believe?

The flavor of faith is not strife and contention. The flavor of faith is *rest.*

In Hebrews 3 and 4, Paul states that the children of Israel never entered into the Promise Land because of their "disobedience." Do you remember what that disobedience was? Did they accidentally eat a pig? Did they complain too much about the quail and manna?

Their disobedience had nothing to do with golden calves or pig barbeques. They didn't enter the land because of their *unbelief*. They were disobedient to the requirement of faith.

But next, Paul goes into a profound passage. He says to be careful that you are not like those unbelieving Israelites ... be careful that you don't fail to *enter into His rest* (Heb. 4:1). Rest is directly correlated to *believing*. Your number one "work" is to rest and trust in the Lord.

*For we also have had the gospel preached to us, just as they did; but the message they heard was of no value to them, because those who heard did not combine it with faith. **Now we who have believed enter that rest** (Heb. 4:2-3, NIV).*

How did the Israelites have the "gospel" preached to them? That was thousands of years before the birth of Christ. The Promise Land was a type and a shadow of Christ. But it seemed too good to be true that it was theirs. Does it seem too good to be true that God gave you all of Himself as a free gift? Let Him shower you with that revelation. That is how faith is imparted to you ... by *hearing this word*.

So faith comes from hearing, that is, hearing the Good News about Christ (Rom. 10:17, NLT).

Jesus also said, "Already you are clean because of the word that I have spoken to you" (John 15:3, ESV). It is hearing this *good news* that activates faith in its validity.

Let the centrality of Christ's cross be your continual source of greater faith. Let the words on this page infuse you with faith. The gospel was originally called *good news* for a reason. It was something people wanted to be part of. Not just an induction into a morality club, or a community ethics improvement class. God forbid! It is total union with an eternally glorious, happy God. A resting in the reality that warfare, strife and darkness are a thing of the past.

Idol of the Will

Again, the flavor of faith is *rest*. Not willpower. This was a core, lifelong message of Martin Luther. His book *Bondage of the Will* was a cornerstone for the Reformation. All the major reformers – Calvin, Zwingli, etc. agreed with him in his battle against the idol of the will.

The *free will* of man sounds like a romantic idea, because we love the concept of liberty. When we think of free will, we think of Braveheart and Independence Day and running through fields of flowers! But the so-called *free will* is not so quixotic.

The human will is one of the biggest idols of the church. Will power fuels religion.

All the Israelites exercised an independent will apart from God and they died out in the desert. Yes, you have a human will. But it is not "free" apart from Him. You cannot even force yourself to be a son of God. When you were born-again, you were *born* a son. You didn't choose Him, He chose you. In the same way, you don't climb yourself into Kingdom miracles or mystical powers. It's all a gift of grace showered on us.

Children of God are those, *"Who are born, not of blood, **nor of the will of the flesh, nor of the will of man, but of God"** (John 1:13, DRB).

Of His own will *He brought us forth by the word of truth, that we should be a kind of firstfruits of His creatures* (Jas. 1:18, ESV).

If you really want to get technical about it, you were not even saved because of your "decision for Christ" but because of His "decision for you." You were in His heart and imagination from before the world was created. He is the Lamb that was slain from the foundation of the world.

*Blessed be the God and Father of our Lord Jesus Christ, who hath blessed us with all spiritual blessings in heavenly places in Christ: according as He **hath chosen us in Him before the foundation of the world**, that we should be **holy and without blame** before Him in love: Having **predestinated** us unto the adoption of children by Jesus Christ to Himself, **according to the good pleasure of His will**, to the praise of the Glory of His grace, wherein He hath made us accepted in the beloved. ... Having made known unto us the **mystery of His will**, according to His good pleasure which **He hath purposed** in Himself. ... In whom also we have obtained an inheritance, **being predestinated according to the purpose of Him who worketh all things after the counsel of His own will** (Eph. 1:3-6, 9, KJV).*

Now, when I read the above passage, I don't see my own will in there one iota. It's all about *His predetermination, His will and His accomplishment.* If the so-called "free" will even exists, who would want it? What are you going to choose apart from God? You have been grafted completely into His will. Now, His Spirit owns and possesses you. Paul called himself a *doulos* – a slave – in fact, he was a *slave to love*. He was ruled and overmastered by the love of God.

Again, we are *without* a will per se. But our will is always subject to the entity that has taken up residence in us. As a new creation, Norman Grubb says, "God changes our 'want,' and the will follows spontaneously. Once God has captured our wills by drawing us back to Himself through Christ, then it is He in us who 'wills and does of His good pleasure. ...'"[45]

It would be a fearful thing to trust in our own efforts. Charles Spurgeon gives us a brilliant statement:

... and I will go as far as Martin Luther, in that strong assertion of his, where he says, "If any man doth ascribe of salvation, even the very least, to the free will of man, he knoweth nothing of grace, and he hath not learnt Jesus Christ aright." It may seem a harsh sentiment; but he who in his soul believes that man does of his own free will turn to God, cannot have been taught of God, for that is one of the first principles taught us when God begins with us, that we have neither will nor power, but that He gives both; that He is "Alpha and Omega" in the salvation of men.[46]

A Sovereign Union

You were not saved or chosen by your willpower. Nor do you maintain that salvation by will. Nor do you add to it virtue or supernatural prowess by will. Never can

---

[45] Norman Grubb, "Romans 7." (Sermon recording).

[46] Charles Spurgeon, "Free Will a Slave." (1855 Sermon).

we boast in self. Paul makes mention of Jacob and Esau in Romans 9, noting that God had predetermined their courses before they were even born.

Before the children had come into existence, or had done anything good or bad, in order that God's purpose and His selection might be effected, not by works, but by Him whose purpose it is (Rom. 9:11, BAS).

God didn't just pick Jacob because he was good and Esau was bad. Jacob was as equally sinful and fallen as Esau – they were both sons of Adam. Jacob's name even meant *schemer, scoundrel, cheat!*

It wasn't Jacob's wrestling that got him the promise land. It was when he lay down and rest his head that God actually showed up and said, "I am the Lord, the God of your father Abraham and the God of Isaac. I will give you and your descendants the land *on which you are lying"* (Gen. 28:13, NIV). Not the land on which he was toiling under Laban in slave labor. Not the land on which he was wrestling. No, it was the land on which he was *lying*. Jacob was clothed not in his own efforts, but his elder brother's garments.

Jacob was loved because God chose to love him. That's all.

Must we wrestle for a blessing like Jacob? Jesus did say that the violent take the Kingdom by force. But there was only one King violent enough to accomplish that. You enter not by warfare, but by inheritance.

People don't like to go down this road of thought because the sovereignty of God over the human will brings up all manner of questions on the origins of evil, Calvinism versus Armenianism, etc. Those are like theological dogs chasing their own tails, and that is not my intent. Of that debate, C.S. Lewis said, "I suspect it is really a *meaningless* question."[47] The intent is not to make us anal and introspective over whose will is this and whose will is that. "What is God" versus "what is me?" There is no longer separation – you are in union.

But at the end of the day, everyone must ultimately learn to *rest* in the sovereignty of God and not *fear* it.

John Piper says, "It won't help if God is good and helpless. It will only help if God is good and sovereign."[48]

C.S. Lewis had a great way of summing up some otherwise seemingly contradictory points:

> *I find the best plan is to take the Calvinist view of my own virtues and other people's vices; and the other view of my own vices and other people's virtues. But tho' there is much to be puzzled about, there is nothing to be worried about. It is plain from Scripture that, in whatever sense the Pauline doctrine is true, it is not true in any sense which excludes its (apparent) opposite. You know what Luther said: 'Do you doubt if you are chosen? Then say your prayers and you may conclude that you are.*[49]

Some think that an over-emphasis on God's sovereignty and a diminishing of the human will blames God for evil. Rest in this: God is sovereign, but He is also

---

[47] C.S. Lewis, *Yours, Jack: Spiritual Direction from C.S. Lewis* (New York: Harper One, 2008), 186.

[48] John Piper, "How Shall People be Saved?" (Aug. 31, 2003 Sermon).

[49] C.S. Lewis, *Letters of C.S. Lewis* (San Diego: Harcourt, Brace and Co., 1966), 433.

good. Rather than blame Him for sickness and trials, let us *believe* Him for healing and deliverance. He doesn't dirty your water, but in His sovereignty, He changes it into wine.

Others fear that if we depend too much on a theology of election, and negate the human will to choose God, then we likewise blame Him for destining some for hell. The only way that some feel to avoid this dilemma is to run toward a namby-pamby universalism. Universalists believe that Jesus died for everyone, and whether they receive Him or not, everyone goes to Heaven. I like Robert Capon's take on the matter:

> *I am and I am not a universalist. I am one if you are talking about what God in Christ has done to save the world. The Lamb of God has not taken away the sins of some — of only the good, or the cooperative, or the select few who can manage to get their act together and die as perfect peaches. He has taken away the sins of the world — of every last being in it — and He has dropped them down the black hole of Jesus' death. On the cross, He has shut up forever on the subject of guilt: "There is therefore now no condemnation. ..." All human beings, at all times and places, are home free whether they know it or not, feel it or not, believe it or not.*

> *But I am not a universalist if you are talking about what people may do about accepting that happy-go-lucky gift of God's grace. I take with utter seriousness everything that Jesus had to say about hell, including the eternal torment that such a foolish non-acceptance of His already-given acceptance must entail. All theologians who hold Scripture to be the Word of God must inevitably include in their work a tractate on hell. But I will not — because Jesus did not — locate hell outside the realm*

*of grace. Grace is forever sovereign, even in Jesus'
parables of judgment.*

Union Being

The first time you glanced at Christ in faith, you saw
that all of your iniquities were taken away. Just as the
Israelites were commanded to look up at the serpent
on the pole in the wilderness, all of their sickness and
infirmities were instantly dissolved. Moses didn't tell
them to suck the poison out of their wounds, or to suck
it out of each other's wounds. Just glance at the tree.

*Just as Moses lifted up the snake in the desert, so
the Son of Man must be lifted up* (John 3:14, NIV).

You don't force yourself into belief. You can't forcibly
retain your Christianity. A dog doesn't force himself to
be a dog. A tree doesn't force itself to be a tree. Holiness is who you are. Union is the essence of your being. You have been transformed with one glance.

You are a child of God. This is effortless. God is not
sitting up in Heaven, forcing Himself to be God. *"Gotta
be God! Gotta be God! Gotta be God!"* The Montgomery New Testament speaks of Jesus, *"who, though
from the beginning He had the nature of God did not
reckon equality with God something to be **forcibly re-
tained"** (Phil. 2:5-6, MON).

Jesus isn't forcing Himself to be God. He just is.

Have you walked in fear that you must *keep yourself* or
somehow labor to maintain your identity in God? I
would encourage you to trust Him with the reins of your
spirituality. You can't force your union with Christ anymore than you can dissolve it.

MYSTICAL UNION

The Substitute

The Galatian bewitchment prompts you to reaccomplish what Christ has already done. But it also overemphasizes a need either to *assist* Christ or *imitate* Him as a model.

Jesus did not come to be your example. He came as your *substitute*.

A couple decades ago, it was trendy for Christians to wear WWJD bracelets – they posed the question, *"What Would Jesus Do?"*

I can answer that question for you right now, so you won't have to wear the bracelet anymore. *Jesus would do what you could never do!*

Different religions see Jesus as a moral teacher, a guide, a prophet or a miracle worker that you should emulate. But He did not bring a formula or model for you to repeat. He stepped into your place and bore the bullet that was yours to take. He *became you and died as you*. Charles Spurgeon writes:

> This gracious system of representation and substitution, which moved Justin Martyr to cry out, "O blessed change, O sweet permutation!" this, I say, is the very groundwork of the gospel of our salvation, and is to be received with strong faith and rapturous joy. In every place the saints are perfectly one with Jesus.[50]

Genesis 4:1 says that the first child born from Adam and Eve was Cain, then next came Abel. But after Cain

---

[50] Spurgeon, "Bands of Love or Union to Christ."

164

THE GALATIAN BEWITCHMENT

murdered his brother, Adam and Eve had a third son named Seth. *Seth* means "substitute" – he was a replacement son. He was prophetic of one to come. Jesus came from the line of Seth.

Though He may allow you fellowship in them at times, stop seeing the sufferings of Christ as something you are called to *imitate*. He suffered *for you*. Embrace humility and admit your need for Jesus to become your substitute in all things.

He became sin so you could be holy.
He was broken so you could be whole.
He was a man of sorrow, so you could have joy.
He was bruised for your iniquity.
He fasted so you could feast.
By His stripes, you were healed.
He bore poverty, so you could righteously prosper.
He felt orphaned so you could be adopted as sons.

Let us begin to see Him not so much as a teacher or moral guide, but as one who stepped in and took our place.

"We have conceived of the Christian life as an imitation of Christ. It is not an imitation of Christ. It is a participation in Christ," said F.J. Huegel. "For we have become partakers of Christ"[51]

The law put us under condemnation, but Christ took that condemnation away. He changed places with us; He put Himself under that condemnation (Gal. 3:13, WPE).

---

[51] F.J. Huegel, *Bone of His Bone* (Fort Washington: CLC Publications, 2006). Quoted in Frank Viola, *From Eternity to Here: Rediscovering the Ageless Purpose of God* (Colorado Springs: David Cook, 2009).

He is most glorified when you receive what He has done for you. He did not say, "This is the cup of the New Covenant, now go tread some more grapes." He simply said, "Drink ye all of it" (Matt. 26:27-28). Your job description is not helper, assistant or even co-laborer as much as it is *drinker*. As John Piper often says, God is most glorified in you when you are most satisfied in Him.

The great old-time preacher Norman Grubb seemed to grasp this substitution at a deep level. He went so far as to say he had been "replaced" by Christ! Of course, Galatians 2:20 does not suggest a pantheistic amalgamation of our personality. But it is a very real statement that *you no longer live, yet Christ lives in you.* You operate by *God's* will power.

"I don't talk in terms of disobedience or obedience when I know who I am," Grubb said. "If this life consists of God in me, it says that God works in me to *will and do of His good pleasure.* ... It's a great life. I don't do anything unless I'm willed and made to. It's great fun."[52]

---

[52] Norman Grubb, "Romans 7." (Sermon recording).

As a Christian, you have already crossed over the River Jordan that separates the wilderness from the Promise Land. Just as Christ was baptized into that river, so were you plunged into His death. You have left the dry places behind. You now have permanent residence in this new land of enchantment. Jesus Christ is the land flowing with milk and honey.

> *For in view of the fact that we are those who have become **permanently united** with Him with respect to the likeness of His death, certainly also we shall be those who as a logical result have become **permanently united** with Him with respect to the likeness of His resurrection* (Rom. 6:5, WET).

You are now sharing in *Jesus'* relationship with the Father. Both in depth and permanence. That is a privilege infinitely too great to comprehend. You are in perma-glory. No speed bumps. No road blocks. Nothing holds you back or stands in your way.

> *For by the death He died He once for all ended His relation to sin, and by the life He now is living He lives in **unbroken relation** to God* (Rom. 6:10, WMS).

> *We perceive that our old identity was co-crucified together with Him. This concludes that the vehicle that accommodated sin in us was scrapped and rendered entirely useless. Our slavery to sin has come to an end. If nothing else stops you from doing something wrong, death certainly does. Faith sees us joined in His death and alive with Him in His resurrection. It is plain for all to see that death lost its dominion over Christ in His resurrection, He*

*need not ever die again to prove a further point. His appointment with death was a once-off. As far as sin is concerned, He is dead. This is the final testimony of the fact that sin's power over man is destroyed. Now it is all life as far as God is concerned. His life reveals an **uninterrupted union** with the life of God* (Rom. 6:6-10, MIR).

A New Kind of Prophet

The age of the wilderness prophet is over. Moses is dead. The law is fulfilled. The Lord is now releasing a company of people who prophesy from a Promise Land perspective. Not just pumping people up with a far-off talk about coming breakthroughs, future revivals or shadows of things to come.

The things to come are already here in Christ and are having their manifestation through us. The New Testament prophet chiefly points *backward* to the breakthrough that has already been achieved. He awakens people to the reality of what Christ has fully accomplished on the cross.

The people lack nothing, except a realization of what they already possess. The Spanish NIV translation of Jesus' words *it is finished* is beautiful. *Todo se ha cumplido* literally means "everything" is finished. *Everything.*

The prophetic movement that has grown over the past few decades is still extremely young. While there have always been prophetic streams in the church, they have a very disjointed lineage. The present move is no different. Rather than coming from a clear line of succession, it sort of started as a pop phenomena in the church. As in many earlier revivals, folks just started stumbling into the reality that God still speaks. The excitement spread, but they didn't have a theological grid for it.

Without any examples to learn from, this new prophetic movement assumed that God still speaks the same way He did in the past – through examples they saw in the Old Testament. Mostly it's a "God's gonna do this" and "God's gonna do that" sort of future telling. And since most of the church lacks a basic revelation on the finished works, these amateur prophets missed the fact that the entire Old Testament had been fulfilled in Christ.

A lot of prophets have run off half-cocked, asking God to reaccomplish stuff He's already done.

Of course God still speaks, but we can't interpret Him without a good Pauline lens on the finished work of the cross. And so what you have today, are a lot of people pulling from *Old Testament* prophetic paradigms. They think they're cutting edge because they are "prophesying" but they're often two thousand years behind the curve. They tell of future goodies, without realizing that those packages have already arrived. *You are the future.* If you are into the prophetic, I would challenge you to read only the letters of Paul for about a year and see how much your perspective changes. Ours is the day that the prophets of old longed to look into – when a people live in unobstructed union with God.

The Old Testament prophet points out the sins of the people. The New Testament prophet points to righteousness of Jesus inside you.

The Old Testament prophet speaks from Mt. Sinai. The New Testament prophet speaks from Mt. Zion.

The Old Testament prophet tells you hope is coming. The New Testament prophet tells you your hope has come.

They say financial breakthrough is on its way. We say it's here.

They say healing is in His wings. We say those wings have touched down.

They ask for revival. We are revival.

They ask for open Heaven. We carry it.

Infinite Glory

I would encourage you to avoid prophets who continuously speak of future coming breakthroughs – especially the ones who give you steps to achieve them! The frequency and flavor of the gospel always inspires you and infuses you with the joyous reality that Christ has accomplished all. It never puts limits, restrictions or conditions on your relationship with God, based on performance. *It is finished* means *it is finished*. And manifestation belongs to those who believe it.

We are a people who have arrived at our destination. Even Heaven is not a future-coming thing. You don't enter Heaven when you die. You entered Heaven two thousand years ago when He died. Don't see Heaven simply as a *place you go*, but as an atmosphere that is already at hand.

Likewise, if you've ever received a prophecy that God will require deserts, dry seasons and difficult breakings to bring you "closer" into union with Him, I would like to set you free from that non-prophet prophecy! Jesus went into the wilderness for you. You are not bound by good seasons and bad seasons. The bondage of the seasons has been broken. You now live in an eternal *year of favor.*

If you anticipate hard times, then negative faith will give you those expectancies.

In the old days, people were bound by the ups and downs of seasons, just as they were bound to the ups and downs of their performance of the law. The sons of Issachar needed to know the times and seasons of the Lord, because men were under a Levitical order. Seasons fluctuated based on their legal performance.

The writer of Hebrews tells us that a new order has come. We are now in the order of Melchizedek – based not on the regulation of the law, but on the eternal power of resurrection life. How is this relevant to you? Well, you don't need to get flustered anymore over "seasonal" prophecies. It's really, really popular for prophets to say, "2014 will be a good year. But 2015 will be a bad year!" They like to mesmerize and sound important by predicting seasonal happenings. It's OK to say God will do *this* or *that.* But you are not blown about by the cosmic winds of chance, based on someone's annual prophetic report.

There is no longer a dry season for *you.* You can call every single year the *year of the favor of the Lord!* You've been ordained for it. You've been called to herald an everlasting season of joy that is outside of time and space – a joy and prosperity that is not based on circumstance. The world may be going to hell in a hand basket, but that is not your portion. Ten thousand may fall at your side, but it won't affect you. You're a good news agent. Never let someone convince you that God is happy with you one day, then out to spank you another day. He always sees His Son in you. And His Son bore your chastisement.

Like the Tree of Life in Heaven, bearing fruit in and out of season, Christ broke the bondage of time for you.

What About Dark Nights and Deserts?

In reading the mystics, we are often taught that the soul must undergo a purging through dark nights of the soul or desert seasons in order to achieve mystical union.

God is not interested in giving you a desert. When we pray, "your Kingdom come ... on Earth as it is in Heaven," we are not asking for a big torture chamber to come down. There is not a vast, dry Sahara in the sky. Yes, your life's calling may see its share of ordinary difficulties. I am not here to tell you life is always perfectly easy. But you are not being progressively "purged" of sin. Even if you're having a tough time, God's portion for you is supernatural joy and peace in the midst of it. He'll use tough times to bless you even more!

We have such a suffering focus in the church. But the appeal of the gospel is always toward an unspeakable joy and weighty Glory in the *midst* of trials – not a value on the trials themselves.

You can have a dark night if you want one, but they are unnecessary. I want to explain this a bit, because it is a common question we receive. The traditional church mystics did put a bit of focus on purging, dry seasons, etc. as means of entering into union. While I love the mystics' focus on the love of God and their ecstatic experiences, I also have a very important filter in place when I read their writings. I never bite off their formulas, depression, false humility or bad theology. I never bite off anyone's system of ascent. We often use the term "new mystics" to describe the current resurgence of mystical Christianity. The reason for this is because we now have five hundred years of grace theology behind us. We don't appeal to our effort or experience to draw us closer to God as many of the old mystics did.

Let me give you an example of how God may use a desert. In Song of Solomon chapter one, we see the bride as she is laboring in the vineyards of her mother's sons. And those sons were angry with her. Meanwhile *her own* vineyard of intimacy with the Lord has been neglected.

My mother's sons were angry with me and made me take care of the vineyards; my own vineyard I have neglected (Song of Sol. 1:6b, NIV).

I believe this represents the sons of mother church roping her into their own agendas. She has been working and toiling under other men's visions – striving under other men's goals and programs. She has been laboring and is exhausted under the heat of the sun. But her own secret place with the Lord – her own garden of fruitfulness has been left unattended.

Have you ever felt this way? Like you got busy with works and religion, but neglected the place of first love? This is a common feeling for many who have neglected their vineyard. Sometimes we need a vineyard restoration program to get back to that place of enjoying personal intimacy in the Lord's presence. If we choose to have a "work and toil" relationship with religion, but neglect the bliss of the secret place, the Lord will gladly allow us a desert to help us out.

*Therefore I am now going to allure her; I will **lead her into the desert** and speak tenderly to her.*

*There I will **give her back her vineyards**, and will make the Valley of Achor* (lit. *trouble*) *a door of hope* (Hos. 2:14-15, NIV my notes).

Deserts can be used to point us back to intimacy. But the desert itself is not the goal. Anywhere outside of the enjoyment of God is going to be dry. Whether you have a desert or not is irrelevant to God. Desert or no desert is not the issue. He wants intimacy and trust. Here is the very thing He is looking for:

Who is this coming up from the desert leaning on her lover? (Song 8:5, NIV)

He wants to see you leaning fully on Him! Resting completely on His finished work. No longer striving or even standing on the strength of your own legs. That is always the position of *coming out* of the desert. I don't have a desert theology anymore. Just a "getting out" theology!

"Do-it-yourself" equals desert. You who are married to Grace, why would you commit adultery with the law? He will let you try that out for as long as it takes until you give up your pride and take the easy way!

Christianity is perfectly easy or perfectly impossible. It depends on who's running the ship.

Isaiah chapter 35 speaks of the coming days of this present New Covenant people. It says that even the burning sands of the desert will turn into bubbling pools. If you're in a desert right now, just cheer up! See it as a wonderful opportunity to become a sprinkler system. You get to turn the place into a garden! There are no deserts this side of the Jordan River. You are an oasis. You have rivers of living water flowing from within your inmost being.

I simply don't believe in deserts anymore. They are for those who refuse to trust. Even the mystics called the dark night the "night of faith." In their limited concept of faith-justification, they still knew that dry times were places to stop striving and to start trusting. Deserts are great places to stop trusting your emotions as a barometer for relationship. In other words, don't rely on the rollercoaster of feeling to dictate whether or not God is happy with you. Just let go and trust. Whether you feel it or not, you have to relax and know He is there. And He's in a good mood!

In the Old Covenant, the people never entered into the Promise Land goodies. By continually leaning on their own fears, they confirmed their lack of trust. This unbelief was counted as disobedience. They continually did loops in the desert until that entire unbelieving generation died off, their bodies strewn across the wilderness. They could not trust that God really had something *too good to be true* for them!

Renowned 17th century theologian Jeremy Taylor once quipped, *"God threatens terrible things if we will not be happy."*

If we won't respond to the kiss, then we'll have to respond to the spank.

Did you know that God never wanted to be harsh with the Israelites? God wanted them to prosper, but the Israelites couldn't believe the goodness. No matter how many miracles He performed, they still thought He brought them out of Egypt just to kill them in the desert. They believed God was a hard taskmaster. Finally, He essentially told them, "Fine, I will be toward you whatever you believe about me." He literally said, "I will do to you the very things I heard you say" (Num. 14:28,

NIV). And so He let them die, just as their negative expectancies of God had dictated.

You will get out of God what you believe about Him. Believe He is harsh and that's what will manifest in your life. Believe He is good and you will experience His goodness. *Let it be according to thy faith.*

Try your best to exaggerate God's goodness. He is always better than your wildest imagination.

Later, the next generation of Israelites did pass into the land. The Lord mystically parted the Jordan River for them – and just as Elijah mystically parted it open for Elisha. Christ's death (symbolized by your shared baptism in the Jordan with Him) supernaturally paved a way through the grave realm for you. It opened access for you into the fullness of God. It bulldozed an uninterrupted open Heaven for you.

Isaiah 35 continues to say that this blossoming wasteland bursts into bloom – and a *highway* will be there. The Highway of Holiness. This is your new multi-million-lane interstate between Heaven and Earth. Not just a little crack in the sky. Jesus paved an open-heaven highway so big for you that you'll never have a dry day again. Realize that the atmosphere of Heaven is zipping through you continually. Your daily portion is to be drunk with love in this garden of delight.

Faith and Love

Until now, we have focused primarily on seeing our union by means of *faith*. That is, by trusting in Christ's accomplished work we perceive this union. But we will now turn to a most important, critical element in this equation. This is a union of *love*. Love is not really taught, but caught. Just as faith is imparted through "hearing the word of God," so does love begin to strangely burn in our heart when we hear this extravagant message of grace. Charles Spurgeon writes:

Love has a most potent power in effecting and sustaining union, but never does it display its force so well as when we see it bringing the Maker into oneness with the creature, the divine into alliance with the human. This, then, is to be regarded as the day-spring of union — the love of Christ Jesus the Lord embracing in its folds the whole of the elected family.[53]

We must see that Christ Himself is the *unio mystica* between God and man. And Holy Spirit is that kiss of union between Christ and His bride.

For a moment, we will explore mystical union through two different lenses. One is the union of faith. John Calvin, Martin Luther and the reformers best exemplify this view. From this perspective, our justification through the work of the cross is the very thing that joins us completely to God. For the reformed mind, salvation and union are essentially the same.

This is right.

On the other hand, the mystics of the church tend to think of union in terms of the experiential *love* of God. Bernard of Clairvaux, Teresa of Avila and other mystics of the church use a language of love. Their writings reference Song of Solomon. They speak much of the practice of God's presence, and contemplation is regarded as a highest aim. Theirs is less a theological paradigm than it is a love song.

------

[53] Spurgeon, "Bands of Love or Union to Christ."

This too is right.

The principles of faith and love have – for various reasons – divided the reformers and the mystics into two separate camps over the centuries. But this should not be so. Faith and love work in tandem. They are inseparable.

"If Bernard's notion of union with God (or Christ) revolves around love, Calvin's surely revolves around faith," writes Dennis Tamburello in *Union with Christ*, where he explores and compares the reformers and the mystics on this subject.[54] Of course, faith and love are both essential elements in the lives of reformers and the mystics alike – this is not a strict categorization. But we must see how faith and experiential love are both essential elements of our union.

Are we through faith or by love? Yes.

A man must *believe* in his *heart*.

We do not define faith as a mere *cognitive* or mental acceptance of Christ's work. It is not an intellectual adherence to the principles of salvation. You are not "saved by knowledge." That is *gnosticism*. Faith is never divorced from the heart.

Faith is Trust

If I have not yet spelled it out in simple English, allow me to define faith:

Faith is trust.

---

[54] Tamburello, *Union with Christ*, 85.

God imparts this ability to trust Him as a gift. And love, too, is a gift. It is not your ability to love Him with your fickle human emotions that counts. It is His own infinite love toward you that saved you. Love is best defined as Jesus hanging on a tree.

No reformer can climb into Heaven through his intellect. No mystic can climb into Heaven through his loftiest, transcendent experiences.

Heaven came down, and we *believe in His love.*

> *And we have seen and had* **faith in the love which God has for us.** *God is love, and everyone who has love is in God, and God is in him* (1 John 4:16, BAS).

We have *faith in love.* In other words, I must *trust* in God's love for me.

Jesus didn't just die for the legal ramifications of justice toward sin. He had to vent His inexhaustible *love* on the cross. He made Himself vulnerable toward us – putting Himself completely out there so that we could trust Him. How could you not trust someone who loves you to such an extreme?

I believe that faith and love are inseparable virtues. Faith is not just an invisible force to bless your finances or heal your body. If you want to know what faith is most like, then look at *love.* And love always *trusts.* Let us turn again to Spurgeon, who says:

> *Faith is the grace which perceives this union, and proceeds from it as its firstfruit. It is, to use a metaphor from the Canticles, the neck which joins the body of the Church to its all-glorious Head. ... Here then is established a living, sensible, and delightful*

179

union which casts forth streams of love, confidence, sympathy, complacency, and joy, whereof both the bride and bridegroom love to drink.[55]

It is by faith that you drink in His love.

For in Christ Jesus neither circumcision nor uncircumcision has any value. **The only thing that counts is faith expressing itself through love** (Gal. 5:6, NIV).

True faith always finds its expression through love.

Is your faith producing love? Does it cause you to love God and man more? If not, maybe you've been trying too hard to be a *believer.* Paul did say to "examine yourselves to see if your faith is genuine. Test yourselves. Surely you know that Jesus Christ is among you; if not, you have failed the test of genuine faith" (2 Cor. 13:5, NLT). Check your love levels. Check your joy levels – see if you're a believer.

Remember, the flavor of faith is not strife, but rest. Maybe you should just relax and trust Him and let Him shower His own love over you. Drink in His infinite acceptance over you. It's impossible to generate love on your own. It only flows freely when you effortlessly bask in His acceptance.

We love because He first loved us (1 John 4:19, NIV).

Want to grow in your ability to love? Love only comes from one source. You don't produce it on your own. Let Him continually love on you every day. Because His love flows to you – that is why it then spills out *through*

---

[55] Spurgeon, "Bands of Love or Union to Christ."

you. Never feel guilty about letting the Father lavish you with His sweetness. It's not just optional, but necessary. This is not a seasonal drink of refreshing so you'll be a better evangelist or nursery worker. Drinking is a lifestyle.

Intimacy is Not a Work

Without faith in the gospel, an error is often made – it was common among some mystics. *We strive to love God more.*

One of the biggest misconceptions in the church today is that "love is a verb." This is the title of popular songs and books on the market, but it's inaccurate. Yes, love *does* verbs. Lovers do what He commands, so if you aren't acting right, it's a great indicator that you don't love. But love itself is not a work.

> *Daughters of Jerusalem, I charge you by the gazelles and by the does of the field: Do not arouse or awaken love until it so **desires*** (Song of Sol. 2:7, NIV).

Rather than an action, love should be defined as a *desire* or *enjoyment* of someone.

Action divorced from desire is religion. We are warned about dead works as much as we are warned about idle hands. Jesus said clearly that, "If you love me, you will obey what I command" (John 14:15, NIV). Surely the qualifier of true love is that it manifests in service, just as faith manifests in works.

But truth be told, Mary always picks the best seat in the house. There is something far beyond service that is imparted to us, as we enjoy the unforced rhythms of grace. True love makes our work seem nothing but a

181

mere trifle. An easy byproduct of a new life. You're infused with energy. People around you may say, "Look at how you're serving the Lord!" But you are drunk with love. You didn't notice that you'd lifted a finger. The greatest saints who paid the most tremendous price throughout church history were the same ones who could genuinely say, "It was nothing. I was in love."

Impossible Love

I can never approach my wife and say, "Dear, I have washed the dishes and mowed the lawn for you for twenty years. I don't *enjoy* you, but I have *worked* for you. Therefore, I truly love you." This over-emphasis on self-sacrifice and human effort is so silly that a child could see through it.

Never be bamboozled when the straining, striving crowd comes along chanting, *"We've got to get hungry! We've got to get more passionate for God!"* It's impossible for you to do that. In fact, those words usually mean someone is showing off for you. Don't let them induce you into their hernia-popping tension routines or work you into an emotional frenzy. You don't force yourself into love. Just be satisfied in the reality that God loves you unconditionally. Out of that will flow fruit that *He* produces through you. One of my favorite John Piper quotes is his adaptation of the Westminster Catechism, saying:

God is most glorified in us when we are most satisfied in Him.

Love-union is not about me drumming up love for God, which is impossible. The "first commandment" to love the Lord your God is technically still a *legal* requirement – meaning it falls under the *law*. It was a lawyer who was questioning Jesus about the law in Matthew 22, when this lofty rule was spoken. Sadly, there are tons of law lovers in the church today! People trying to love God just because they are supposed to.

Granted, loving God is definitely the "greatest" commandment. But it is still a *commandment*. It is the grand summation of the law. And we know that law does not save us.

Did you know there is something greater than the greatest commandment? Something bigger and better than loving God?

You are not saved by your love for God. *You are saved by His love for you.* You are not saved by your faith toward God. You are saved by *His grace*, which produces *His faith* in you.

His love for you is greater than the law.

The cross is the fountainhead of all love.

If you won't accept that He accepts you ... if you don't allow Him to wash your feet like Peter ... then you have no part in Him. Only in allowing the Father to pour His love into you, will you ever have love to give back to Him. Until you taste His goodness, love will always be a duty and never a ravenous enjoyment.

The Mystical Marriage

I do not work to become united to my wife. Our union was consummated and sealed on our wedding day. Now, we are in a continual state of enjoying one another. I don't believe the religious lies that tell me marriage is hard work. I would effortlessly lay my life down for my wife because I enjoy her. I thrive on her com-

pany. We cohabitate. Everything I have is hers. The
same is true with the Lord.

Love is the bond that ties us. Spurgeon comments on
this bond of love:

> *The saints were from the beginning joined to Christ
> by bands of everlasting love. Before He took on
> Him their nature, or brought them into a conscious
> enjoyment of Himself, His heart was set upon their
> persons, and His soul delighted in them. Long ere
> the worlds were made, His prescient eye beheld
> His chosen, and viewed them with delight. Strong
> were the indissoluble bands of love which then
> united Jesus to the souls whom He determined to
> redeem. Not bars of brass, or triple steel, could
> have been more real and effectual bonds. True
> love, of all things in the universe, has the greatest
> cementing force, and will bear the greatest strain,
> and endure the heaviest pressure: who shall tell
> what trials the Savior's love has borne, and how
> well it has sustained them? Never union more true
> than this.[56]*

Throw out all the bad theology you've ever heard that
says your wedding to Christ is a *future* thing. Also toss
out all the jargon that says it's your job to spot stain
and iron your own wedding dress. The Blood of Jesus
works wonders on bridal garments. Consummation
happened on the cross. You're hitched. The apostle
says we're flesh of His flesh and bone of His bone.
There's no annulment to that marriage! Now you enjoy
the party. The *wedding supper* is the now and future
continuous celebration feast of love.

[56] Spurgeon, "Bands of Love or Union to Christ."

Consummation does not happen in a series of ecstatic experiences. Many mystics were mistaken in thinking that their contemplative journeys brought them into divine wedlock. Do not labor in mental ascent, trying to present yourself to Him. You enjoy Him *now* as a wedded bride in ecstatic communion. How? Christ toiled for you just as Jacob labored for Rachel.

Marriage is one of the most mystical symbols of our union to God. The mystics used the marital metaphor to describe contemplative experiences, whereas the reformers used marriage to describe the union that flows from faith. Communion is the daily expression of what faith acquires.

The Lord issued Israel a writ of divorce. She was unfaithful. Her marriage contract – the law – was incapable of captivating her heart. But now, we who are Christ's spouse have a better promise. We will never know divorce, for He says, "I will betroth you to me forever" (Hos. 2:19). This word of betrothal is now written on our hearts.

> *After all, no one ever hated his own body, but he feeds and cares for it, just as Christ does the church – for we are members of His body. For this reason a man will leave his father and mother and be united to his wife, and the two will become one flesh. This is a profound mystery – but I am talking about Christ and the church* (Eph. 5:31-32, NIV).

The very reason God instituted the sacrament of marriage – *for this reason* the apostle says – was to illustrate the unio mystica between God and man. The siren of earthly romance is just a *sign* and *remembrance* of a deeper, richer homeward call. Song of Solomon is parabolic of union with Christ that is far more profound than a man and a woman share. Our union with Him is pleasurable. Even the blessed physical merger of natural spouses is indicative of a *higher* pleasure we experience in ecstatic unio mystica. Yet our union with God is utterly *trans-sexual* – in this I define the word as meaning "beyond sexual." Our relation with the Lord is more exalted and higher than the human senses or physical sexuality could begin to conceptualize. Our natural senses alone are not adequate to fully comprehend the eternal weight of this Glory – it is likewise *trans-sensory*.

Of course, we can now enjoy and *feel* His manifest presence, thanks to faith. But your highest and most transcendent experience is still just sniffing the cork, compared to the eternal sea of communion wine offered to you. Understanding this is helpful. We never need to drum up the feelings in order to acquire faith. Feelings and subjective experiences are glorious by-products, not prerequisites to faith.

One Body, One Spirit

In a mystical way, we are one *body* with Christ – flesh of His flesh and bone of His bone. He wears your skin. Actually, we are His *only* body on planet Earth! This is realized in communion when we partake of His real flesh and blood.

"Passing all human union is that mystical cleaving unto the Church, for which Christ did leave His Father, and become one flesh with her," writes Spurgeon.[57]

But beyond the *one flesh* union we share with an earthly spouse, "he who is joined to the Lord is one

UNINTERRUPTED UNION

---

[57] Spurgeon, "Bands of Love or Union to Christ."

186

spirit with Him" (1 Cor. 6:17). Our union is *spirit*, so the seed will endure.

"There is a closer union in this holy marriage than there can be in any other. In other marriages, two make one flesh, but Christ and the believer make one spirit," writes Puritan minister Thomas Watson. "Now as the soul is more excellent than the body, and admits of far greater joy, so this spiritual union brings in more astonishing delights and ravishments than any other marriage relationship is capable of. The joy that flows from the mystic union is unspeakable and full of Glory (I Peter 1:8)."[58]

We get mixed up about the nature of union – physical and spiritual – because of the insufficiency of the mind to comprehend it. John Calvin admitted his own inability to grasp it, writing, "How this happens far exceeds the limits of my understanding, I must confess; thus I have more of an impression of this mystery than I strive to comprehend it." And again he writes, "Let us therefore labour more to feel Christ living in us, than to discover the nature of that communication."[59]

Union entails that we are restored to God's image and participating in His nature, both flesh and spirit. To understand the exact mechanics of how we share in God's substance is not just difficult – *it is unnecessary.* You don't analyze a kiss. You just enjoy it.

We can be sure of this: the constitution of our members is now thoroughly immortal. Consider again Spurgeon's treatise on union:

---

[58] Thomas Watson, *The Godly Man's Picture* (Banner of Truth, 1992).

[59] Calvin, *Institutes.* Quoted in Tamburello, *Union with Christ,* 89.

So that in a twofold sense, the head and members are of one nature, and not like that monstrous image which Nebuchadnezzar saw in his dream. The head was of fine gold, but the belly and the thighs were of brass, the legs of iron, and the feet, part of iron and part of clay. Christ's mystical body is no absurd combination of opposites, the head is immortal, and the body is immortal too, for thus the record stands, "Because I live, ye shall live also." "As is the heavenly, such are they also that are heavenly." "As we have borne the image of the earthy, we shall also bear the image of the heavenly;" and this shall in a few more years be more fully manifest to us, for "this corruptible must put on incorruption, and this mortal must put on immortality." Such as is the head, such is the body, and every member in particular. A chosen Head and chosen members; an accepted Head, and accepted members; a living Head, and living members. If the head be pure gold, all the parts of the body are of pure gold also. Thus there is a double union of nature as a basis for the closest communion.[60]

One Image

A primary aspect of union is the participation and sharing of His *image*.

Mankind was made in His image. Now we have been restored to His image. In fact, you look more like God than Adam did. He's not just walking *with* you in the cool of the day. Now He lives *inside* of you.

To understand this union of substance, body and nature, it may help to return again to Norman Grubb's ex-

---

[60] Spurgeon, "Bands of Love or Union to Christ."

planation of the believer's body as a container for God. Not having an *independent* self that walks alongside of God – rather, *self is an illusion. I no longer live, but Christ lives in me.* There must be an identification of *Christ as you.* He has actually removed the *you* and inserted Himself. You are a suit He wears in the Earth.

Finally, we are members of the body of Christ, and any body operates by the mind and will of the head, and nothing else. It has no body-led activity of its own. So in each case the human is only the agent – as temple, manifesting the presence of the deity; as branch, expressing the nature and producing the fruit of the vine; as body member, set in action by the head; as slave, doing the will of the owner; as wife, bearing the children of the husband; and as vessel, only a container and nothing else.[61]

This merger is so phenomenally inexplicable. It is nearly like attempting to describe the incarnation. The God-man union is never more clearly portrayed than in the birth of Christ.

Blessings of Union

With Christ replacing and possessing the vessel of *self*, every spiritual blessing now flows freely – both invisible and natural. Never compartmentalize the manner in which Christ effuses Himself and His benefits through you. The greatest patriarchs of the Bible possessed spiritual treasuries that were also mirrored in their tangible, outward lives. We are kings and priests. We have spiritual, unseen authority – but also natural kingly authority in the Earth.

---

[61] Norman Grubb, *Yes, I Am* (Blowing Rock, NC: Zerubbabel Press, 1982), 40.

This marital union with Christ provides a brilliant illustration of our dual authority in both Heaven and Earth. Consider how rich a believer is. You are wed to majesty. You have a vested interest in all His treasuries by virtue of this unio mystica. As the king said to Esther His bride, "What would you like? Even if it is up to half of the kingdom, it will be granted to you" (Esth. 5:3).

"On Earth He exercises towards her all the affectionate offices of Husband. He makes rich provision for her wants, pays all her debts, allows her to assume His name, and to share in all His wealth. Nor will He ever act otherwise to her," adds Spurgeon. "Death must sever the conjugal tie between the most loving mortals, but it cannot divide the links of this immortal marriage. In Heaven they marry not, but are as the angels of God, yet is there this one marvelous exception to the rule, for in Heaven Christ and His Church shall celebrate their joyous nuptials."[62]

The abundant blessings of this union are far too many to account. Physical healing. Financial provision. Reconciliation in relationships. Emotional fulfillment. Unspeakable joy. Righteous authority to be wielded over regions and people groups. Creative miraculous abilities. Mystical powers. Authority in this age and the age to come. The possibilities are endless, as you are wed to God.

One of the most amazing aspects of marital union is that of co-habitation. You do not have an infrequent audience with the King. You sit ever with Him enthroned. Just as the husband and wife live together in uninterrupted fellowship, so do we dwell in God's house both now and forevermore. A wife is afforded

---

[62] Spurgeon, "Bands of Love or Union to Christ."

benefit that a stranger could never conceive possible. Watson paints a vivid analogy, for instance, of how this marital union affects the believer on Judgment Day:

In the case of passing sentence at the day of judgment. ... There is a marriage union and, oh Christian, your Husband shall be your judge. A wife would not fear appearing at the bar if her husband was sitting as judge. What though the devil should bring in many indictments against you? Christ will expunge your sins in His blood. Could He possibly say, "I shall condemn my spouse?" Oh, what a comfort this is! The Husband is judge. Christ cannot pass sentence against His spouse without passing it against Himself. For Christ and believers are one.[63]

Manifesting the Fullness

One of the biggest stumbling blocks to the gospel message (from charismatics anyway) revolves around the topic of manifestations. If I am really in effortless union with God, then why don't I levitate every day? Why don't I heal every single person I meet on the street? Why don't I glow like a light bulb?

People often doubt the message, because they are not seeing a particular manifestation. This is one of the most problematic issues for those who want to see more of the supernatural in their lives.

You have to believe in order to see. Don't put the cart before the horse. Believing comes *before* the manifestation. Why are you not levitating every day? Well I can promise you this much ... you're not going to float by

---

[63] Watson, *The Godly Man's Picture.*

adding anything to Christ's work. A powerless life is a symptom of the fall. But be assured that the antidote to this disease will always be the same. Belief in Christ's finished work is the mother lode of all supernatural power and experience. Anyone who tries to enter in by any other door than the Sheep Gate is a thief and a robber.

The most marvelous miracles I have ever seen in my meetings are the ones that accompanied faith in the simple gospel message. From physical levitations to oil running down every wall of the church building – the craziest phenomena are those that flow out of faith in this good news. I have seen thousands of healings – from cancers and tumors to blind eyes, deaf ears and cripples being cured. But I have never taught a single message on healing, nor given any special "mystical knowledge" to help people manifest such things. I simply encourage them to trust in what Christ has done.

Some people do have faith for particular types of things: healings, manifestations of gold dust and feathers, etc. Yet these folks may still give you formulas, lacking a clear understanding of the good news of co-crucified union. For me, the message and the miracle must be inseparable. Trust in Christ's cross as the ultimate and final connection to the Glory realm.

If you aren't seeing a specific type of miracle in your life, continue to have a childlike expectancy for those extraordinary things. But an absence of certain miracles doesn't indicate an absence of union.

You have delegated authority to do the impossible. But sometimes the authority of the believer wrongly trumps the overarching principle of God's sovereignty in the charismatic world. Sometimes, we need to stop pushing so hard for certain types of manifestations, while trusting the Lord in these areas. I love the crazy and exotic ways that God displays His power – and He wants to showcase this stuff more than you want to see it. But for me, manifesting should never become a *work*. It's just believing and being who you are. A light bulb doesn't work to shine. A believer doesn't work to manifest. Signs just follow the believer. I do understand that there are principles of "working" miracles that we can adhere to. But your effortless trust in Christ far outweighs human responsibility to perform.

Check out the Mirror Translation's version of Hebrews 3:19 with its corresponding notes:

... even though (the Israelites) survived by super-natural means in the wilderness for forty years, they failed to grasp what God had in mind for them. Their own unbelief disqualified them. *(You can experience God's supernatural provision and protection and yet remain outside his rest. The ultimate proof of faith is not experience of the supernatural, but entering into his rest. His rest celebrates his perfect work. ... He longs for you to discover your own completeness and perfection as seen from his point of view. His rest is sustained in you by what he sees, knows and says about you in reference to the finished work of Christ.)*

Even Jesus did not levitate every day. Peter's shadow healed the sick, but we don't read of James' shadow doing anything so fancy. Dream for the unusual, but don't put qualifications on how God must demonstrate Himself through you. What would it be like to manifest the fullness of God in your life? Different people have their own unique, subjective definitions of how this should look.

UNINTERRUPTED UNION

If you aren't floating regularly, transporting super-naturally from place to place, or walking on water, don't feel like you are missing out. We want all that God has for us, but you are primarily called to rest in His grace. Desire spiritual gifts, but let your foremost passion be the bliss of His finished sacrifice.

Actually the apostle Paul defined the greatest manifestation as being *love*. He nestles the "love chapter" of 1 Corinthians 13 right between two chapters on spiritual gifts. I have seen lots of miracles and lots of bad character over the years. I am far more impressed with a sincere lover than a self-promoter who can walk through walls.

If you think it's a cop-out to say love is more impressive than a levitation miracle, then consider becoming a Christian.

God's primary nature is not magician. It is *Father*. He is defined foremost by love rather than power. His greatest display of power – the cross – seemed unimpressive to the natural eye. If you are walking in love, you are shining forth the fullness of God to the degree of your age and maturity.

Paul always promoted the miraculous, but only as a proof of the gospel – never at the expense of it.

Experiential Union

The term "mystical union" when used by the church mystics, almost always referred to an *experiential* participation in the divine life. You can also find this in the doctrine of deification – *theosis* – which is prevalent in the Eastern Orthodox Church. There are those in every stream who adhere to some type of experiential process of joining our sensory perceptions to God, or partaking in the divine nature.

Let me be clear about this. We do not come into union with God through experience. Instead, we experience God *because* we are in union with Him. Tamburello points out in his comparison between mystic and reformer, "We are saved by grace through faith; and while contemplative experiences of union are not essential, faith is absolutely essential."

Experience has to be rooted in faith. And faith has to be experienced.

Christian mysticism deals with experiential knowledge of God. Such knowledge is apprehended through subjective interaction – all of which must be rooted in faith. We do not base our theology on subjective experience. Rather, we allow the Word to be our springboard for experiencing the divine.

If the reformers championed faith, the mystics championed experience. But can the two be separated? Faith is the *substance* of things hoped for (Heb. 11:1). True faith always manifests in experience. What a dull relationship would we have, if never we experienced the divine! Spurgeon writes:

*This, which we call **vital union** is rather a matter of experience than of doctrine; it must be learned in the heart, and not by the head. Like every other work of the Spirit, the actual implantation of the soul into Christ Jesus is a mysterious and secret operation, and is no more to be understood by carnal reason than the new birth of which it is an attendant. Nevertheless, the spiritual man discerns it as a most essential thing in the salvation of the soul, and he clearly sees how a living union to Christ is*

UNINTERRUPTED UNION

195

the sure consequence of the quickening influence of the Holy Spirit, and is indeed, in some respects, identical with it.[64]

Experience is in no way a qualifier or pre-requisite for union. But experience *will* follow true faith, because true faith always manifests, works and demonstrates.

I want to be more reformed than the reformers and more mystical than the mystics. I want to believe blindly and love feverishly.

What a chaotic and fearful life if my relationship with God were based on the fickle ups and downs of experience? And what a boring, dull and predictable one if it was altogether void of experience!

When faith in Christ's act of love becomes your solid foundation, you then have a dance floor that can handle your joy. Wave after wave of glorious bliss flows from this unwavering union, sealed with blood. Life becomes an unending expression of the divine, because experience is no longer based on your efforts but His.

The role of Holy Spirit is to make humans participants in the divine life. This union is to be experienced and enjoyed. Holy Spirit is the one who produces manifestations. He is the one who produces fruit. He is the one who brings practical enablement of a holy life. But please, never separate Holy Spirit from the *person* of Christ. This is an undivided Trinity. We must understand that the Paraclete is the *Spirit of Christ*. Let us return to the sure and solid way of a Christocentric Pentecost.

---

[64] Spurgeon, "Bands of Love or Union to Christ."

A Christocentric Pentecost

An emphasis on the finished work of Christ sometimes leads people baffled at the role of Holy Spirit. He is thought of as "Sanctifier" or "Purifier." As we have most thoroughly explained, however, these things have taken place at a finite point on the cross. Never forget that Holy Spirit was released because of the open veil of Christ' broken body.

Let's look at the Spirit's role in union. Our lives are not moving from *sinner to saint*. Our lives are now moving from Glory *to Glory*. There is a massive difference. You are starting on a full tank, and it never runs out.

And we, who with unveiled faces all reflect the Lord's Glory, are being transformed into His likeness with ever-increasing Glory, which comes from the Lord, who is the Spirit (2 Cor. 3:18, NIV).

This verse is not an admission of your present lack. You have already been restored to His image. This verse speaks of a greater and greater manifestation of what you already possess. This transformation literally means "metamorphosis" or "transfiguration."[65] You are already a son, and the world is waiting for the sons to fully manifest the Glory they carry in Christ. Manifestation is not a work. It is an effortless byproduct of believing. Shining forth who you are. We reflect Him best by gazing at Him continually. You can't even hold the gaze on your own – you're locked into a tractor beam of irresistible grace!

---

[65] Strong, *Exhaustive Concordance of the Bible*, Entry 3339.

Holy Spirit is now continually speaking the Good News to you. He is always reminding you of Christ. He is consistently teaching you and renewing your mind to the reality of this New Creation. He effects the manifestation of who you are – He unpackages the image that you already possess. Through revelation of the truth, manifestation and experience unfolds.

It is because you have His nature that you can now manifest it through the power of the Holy Spirit.

"There is one aspect of this subject of natural union which it were improper to pass over in silence, for it is very precious to the believer. While the Lord Jesus takes upon Himself our nature (2 Pet. 1:4), He restores in us that image of God (Gen. 1:27), which was blotted and defaced by the fall of Adam," says Spurgeon. "He raises us from the degradation of sin to the dignity of perfection."[66]

We must redefine unio mystica. The saints have mostly considered the term *mystical union* to be something we progressively receive through contemplative experiences. We have made a strong Biblical case that the point of the gospel was to graft you fully into this union as an instant gift. And yet, we do not deny that there is a process of maturation and growth in this union. Let us look at some ways we grow in our union.

Does Union Grow?

Human language makes feeble attempts at grasping and explaining concepts of union. We talk about getting "closer" to people in the relationships around us. *I'm going to spend some time with the family so we can get*

---

[66] Spurgeon, "Bands of Love or Union to Christ."

closer. This concept of *getting closer* to someone or *growing in love* sometimes fails to appreciate the engrafted nature of our relationship with God. Again, He is like a Siamese twin!

Can one truly get *closer* to God? Has Christ only brought us part way?

Consider the analogy of a vine and a branch. It is impossible for a branch to grow any closer to the vine than it already is. The two are physically connected. There is no breach that is progressively being filled.

Now, does the branch continue to grow? Yes! It even flourishes, buds and bears fruit. But is it growing *toward* union, or *because* of union?

There is forever going to be a glorious exploration and enjoyment of God.

Our affections are continuously being awakened as we drink in the love of Christ. Could we be mistaken to say our hearts are continuously being knitted closer together? Perhaps love is coming alive in us, because we are *one with love.* God doesn't love. *God is Love.*

It is not that our hearts and emotions are being more and more deeply united to Christ. They are tied into the wine vine right now. But love is bursting and flowering out of us now in greater and greater degrees.

It is understandable that people would think this affectionate, emotive and mental absorption of the soul into God is something that increases over time. They are seeing more and more of the *evidence* of God in their soul. But this experiential fruit is a product of a pre-existing union of faith. Now faith is *expressing itself through love.*

Here is a phrase from Bernard of Clairvaux that you will find echoed in a million different ways in the writing of the mystics: *God is love, and the deeper one's union with God, the more full one is of love.*[67]

This quote is sweet and syrupy on the surface, yet it implies that one person's union with God is deeper than another's. This is surely the *partial* truth that is the Achilles heel of the mystics.

You are not falling in love with God. You *fell* into Mr. Love. You are united to Love. Love is a Person. Now, just as the sap flows effortlessly through the vine into the branch, so is there a continual infilling of Holy Spirit – a continual infilling of Love Himself. You grow in Love, just as the branch grows.

Maturing in Union

We acknowledge that a father's faith may be more mature than a child's. But simple, childlike trust is the gold standard in the Kingdom. One has no less access to God than the other. Each is perfect for his age. For this reason, it is foolish for us to compare ourselves one with another. A sapling is the same substance as the mighty oak. One may be more mature than the other, but both are fully and completely still *trees*.

We are all now the same substance and body of Christ. We are all the same substance of holiness, whether sapling or fully grown.

I am not really moving *deeper* into union or getting closer to God. I'm already fully connected to the Head. Our union has been procured. Rather, I am drinking

---

[67] Tamburello, *Union with Christ,* 69.

deeper *from* that very real and complete union that I already have. Enjoying and unwrapping the Gift who is my celestial Spouse.

Although we may use the phrase, "Our family is getting closer," those familial bonds are never broken. We share blood. The more I enjoy my wife, I am not becoming *more married* to her. I am enjoying the marital connection that we already have. Think of your marriage contract as *faith*. It binds you. But marriage without love is just a piece of paper.

Consummation of our mystical marriage with Christ does not happen in an ecstatic experience, nor does it occur in a future heavenly procession. It was on the cross that we bled into one.

Love always grows. The love I have for my wife grows every day. But my union with my wife is not incomplete today, merely because I will love her more tomorrow. I even believe that the love of God is a growing, expanding thing. His Glory always increases.

It is also safe to say that we are drawing closer in a union of *purpose*. Every time I open my Bible, I learn more and more to know His will. In the revealing of His will, my life can better align with His purposes. As a new believer, I may not understand all the plans of God for my life. This does not mean I am incomplete, per se. But to the degree of revelation I have, I am able to fill those shoes more and more by grace.

One could also say we are drawing closer in a union of *personality*. The more time I spend with Him, the more I see what He is like. *When we see Him, we will be like Him* (1 John 3:2). The more His personality is revealed to me, I effortlessly reflect and manifest His nature like a mirror. His nature that I *already* possess.

MYSTICAL UNION

There are innumerable ways in which we mature. Even Jesus matured and grew. But always remember that a process of maturity and growth do not imply a present lack or deficit of godliness.

What I am Not Saying

I want to be clear on this matter, because somebody is still having a hard time swallowing the message. Let me tell you what I am *not saying*. Martin Luther commented, "You are not only responsible for what you say, but also for what you do not say."

I am not saying that Christians do not *mature*. We are also still in a lifelong process of *growing* in revelation and understanding. We are all still learning, and this requires humility and teachability.

Immaturity is not sin. It's OK to act like a toddler if you are a toddler. Immaturity is only wrong when you are thirty-eight years old and still acting like a toddler. Likewise, because you are still a *student* in the process of learning and training, does not make you a sinner.

To say you are perfect in *holiness* does not indicate that you are yet fully grown. And we are all still growing. We will forever grow in the Glory.

The person who says they can sin to their hearts content because they are now "perfect" has not understood a word I have preached from the beginning. Nor am I saying that it is *impossible* for a Christian to sin.

If you are exploiting the grace of God – sinning under the guise of your perfection – please do the rest of us a favor and stop calling yourself a Christian.

UNINTERRUPTED UNION

If the Lord reveals a wrong way of action or thinking in your life, just repent – turn back to faith – and let it go.

What I *am saying* is that repentance is a byproduct of salvation – not its prerequisite. In believing you are made righteous, you will manifest that righteousness. It is a dependent righteousness that flows from being *in Him*. It is a real, tangible God-given God-righteousness.

Clothed with Christ

Ah, what a scandal! My beloved is mine, and I am His. What a boast for a mere mortal to make. Bernard points out that this is not a union of equals:

> There is no doubt that in this passage a shared love blazes up, but a love in which one of them experiences the highest felicity, while the other shows marvelous condescension. **There is no betrothal or union of equals here.**[68]

Apart from the cross, this would be an unequal union indeed. But Christ is not unequally yoked with His bride. The gospel clearly tells us that God has put the fullness of His own worth on you. The fullness of His beauty. All of His power. All of His splendor. The list goes on.

If He gave you anything more, you would be a threat to the Trinity.

Some would try to preserve a distance in the words *likeness* or *equality* between God and man in the mystical union. But even mystics like Bernard attested to

---

[68] Tamburello, *Union with Christ,* 70.

203

UNINTERRUPTED UNION

man's soul being "glorified by its likeness to the Word."[69] There is no problem in claiming deification, as long as we never lose sight of its source.

He condescended only to place you in the highest Heaven. He became flesh that you might be gods.

"Pause here, devout reader, and see if thou canst without ecstatic amazement, contemplate the infinite condescension of the Son of God in thus exalting thy wretchedness into blessed union with His Glory," continues Spurgeon.[70]

You are not a bride whose garments are woven by the hands of men. You are clothed fully in divinity. In robes of His righteousness. There is no god-likeness apart from Him. See how close He is to you. Like the clothes that stick to you, in fact closer than your skin.

You are all sons of God through faith in Christ Jesus, for all of you who were baptized into Christ have clothed yourselves with Christ (Gal. 3:26-27).

Immersed into Christ, you have fallen into deity. My heart for you is that you will never feel naked again. Let your boast be in Him, and never believe the lie that you are stained with the old nature. It is not your job to "put off the old self" and "put on the new self." That verse actually says, "Seeing that you have put off the old man with his deeds; and put on the new man" (Col. 3:9-10, KJV). These words "put on" are *enduo* in the Greek, meaning to *sink into*.[71] Your union with Christ was an effortless sinking into grace.

---

[69] Tamburello, *Union with Christ,* 71.

[70] Spurgeon, "Bands of Love or Union to Christ."

[71] Strong, *Exhaustive Concordance of the Bible,* Entry 1746.

Grafted into Union

As we, the branch, drink in the sweet sap of the Vine –
that nectar being Holy Spirit – fruit just happens. Your
only job is a passive one – *abide*. Rest in faith and
love.

Calvin wrote of this vital experience of abiding. He said,
"Engrafted into the death of Christ, we derive a secret
energy from it, as the shoot does from the root."[72] It is
His divine energy that flows through you, "For it is God
which works in you both to will and to do of His good
pleasure" (Phil. 2:13, AKJV). And again, Paul says he
is "energized by Christ's power that is so mightily at
work within me" (Col. 1:29, TNT).

As much as we speak of effortless Christianity, one
must see that our own lives are full of fruit. I do not per-
sonally wish to boast, just as Paul hated to boast. But
at times, he had to point to his fruit as evidence of
Christ's work. I have seen countless tens of thousands
come to conversion. I have seen untold physical healings and unusual signs and wonders. I regularly wit-
ness creative miracles and prophetic phenomena in the
heavens and on the Earth below. I face consistent persecution from the church and the world and must often
pioneer alone. We see drug and sexual addictions broken and families restored. We are midwives in an entire
ecstatic movement being birthed in the church today.
We plant churches, run orphanages, feeding programs
and crusades all around the world. We run worldwide
magazine, video and internet media publishing. And on
top of it all, I have a healthy family and a fantastic marriage. I work a great many more than 40 hours a week!

---

[72] John Calvin, *Calvin's New Testament Commentaries* (Grand
Rapids: William B. Eerdmans Publishing Co., 1965), 42.

Where is the strife? Where is the need for acceptance before God or men? Not here. The reason for it all is that I am drunk with love. I can't help what I do, because I have a fire burning in my bones.

Does Grace Produce Apathy?

Some would charge that preaching a gospel of grace produces apathy in the church. Preach grace, and people will stop working, they say. This comes from a wrong definition of grace.

Grace has nothing to do with God "hiding" from your sins and letting you get away with stuff. He's not a senile Santa who just puts naughty kids onto the nice list at Christmas. Grace eradicates your sinfulness. It is actually defined as *the divine influence of God on your life*. As an "influence," grace is like a tangible thrust that fills your sails and propels you into action all around the world. It drives and pushes the believer with such a holy and happy ambition, that she will spend herself completely. A lover will do what a hired hand never will.

I am a passive instrument of His grace.

Your union is primarily two-fold in purpose. The first and primary reason He chose you is the simple enjoyment of divine co-habitation. The second is a byproduct of the first – it is to bear the fruit of the Spirit, "That you may be married to another; to Him who was raised from the dead, that we should bear fruit to God" (Rom. 7:4).

The branch can never boast in its own fruit bearing. Fruitfulness is often even an *unintended* byproduct of the pleasures of marital union. My wife and I didn't plan to have all of our kids – most of them came as surprises from our union! In the same way, I can honestly

say that I stumbled into all of our ministry breakthroughs by accident. I was just enjoying Jesus, and
miracles started happening. I boast in Him as the Initia-
tor, the Sustainer and the Finisher.

Our union is effortless. This does not mean we become
idle or lazy. A man who does not work is worse than an
unbeliever. You'll never find a mooching monk. This
new move of gospel-believing ecstatics will see more
fruitfulness than ever before. We are infused with divine energy from our union – a fire that burns in our
bones that has to come out. We cannot help but to
serve and manifest our faith through works. But it is
Christ who is *working through us*, according to His
good pleasure. Faith without works is dead. We don't
work for faith. Faith works through us.

Right living and good deeds are the fruit of faith, not its
prerequisites.

Remember also that fruit is not just about deeds, so
never compare or feel inferior to someone else's outward successes. This is the true fruit that the Spirit
produces through the spouse: *love, joy, peace, long-
suffering, gentleness* – for as Thomas Watson says,
"barrenness is a shame in Christ's spouse."[73]

God is not looking for workers, but for lovers. And the
lovers will outwork the workers in these days.
I do not preach much about working. That's one area
where actions should speak louder than words. I
preach on work by using my hands.

The definition of "work" however, has changed for us.
Like Adam, a new creation is now tending the Garden

---

[73] Watson, *The Godly Man's Picture.*

of Pleasure. Our chief end is toward the enjoyment of God in the midst of our vocation. In divine union, work and play should rise to meet together as one. This is your *calling*.

"To me, work that does not rise to the level of play is flawed work and play that is simply an escape from the expenditure of effort is flawed play," says Capon. "Play is the sovereign category, not work. If we have any final vocation, any ultimate calling, it is into that play."[74]

A Final Thought

You have one life to live. Don't waste it trying to become something. Whatever you do in life runs the risk of turning into that treadmill of religion, as long as we're duped into thinking identity is a future destination. Go ahead and have a good identity crisis right now, get it out of the way, and decide that you *are who you are*. Something new. You are no longer your own. You're betrothed to another. You've taken *His* identity, and that's good enough to get you into any VIP lounge on the planet.

Then grab all that time wasted trying to prove yourself – worrying, fretting, formulating and polishing up the corpse that *once was you* – and go use it to take over the world for Jesus. Why? *Just for the fun of it.* Nothing can stop you. The possibilities are endless in this new realm of union. And above all ... *keep the feast.*

---

[74] Capon, *Health, Money & Love and Why We Don't Enjoy Them*, 139.

ABOUT THE AUTHOR

John Crowder and his wife, Lily, have a passion to spread the supernatural gospel of Jesus Christ in its exuberant love and joy. They have four children. The Crowders are revivalists based in Santa Cruz, CA. where they have planted a thriving local church community with friends. As founders of Sons of Thunder Ministries and Publications, they speak at events around the world. Along with thousands of articles, John has authored four books:

The New Mystics
The Ecstasy of Loving God
Seven Spirits Burning
Mystical Union

John and Lily long to release a creative new movement of ecstatic believers, who are enthralled by the finished works of Christ and who demonstrate miraculous lifestyles. Their heart is to see the Kingdom of God invade every sector of society. John has a vision to equip a supernatural generation to walk in the Glory – clearly communicating the finished work of the cross and operating in signs, wonders and the wine of divine intimacy needed for the last-day harvest.

Sons of Thunder plants children's homes for orphans and hosts evangelism campaigns, conferences and schools across the globe. Creative miracles and unusual signs and wonders mark John's ministry.

CONNECT WITH US

There are many ways to stay connected with us!

Visit us online at:
WWW.THENEWMYSTICS.COM

Find out about conferences, mission trips, schools, teaching resources, John's itinerary and more.

Email us at:
info@thenewmystics.org

Write us at:
P.O. Box 3591
Santa Cruz, CA 95063

Call us toll-free:
1-877-343-3245

Subscribe to John Crowder's magazine, *The Ecstatic*
www.TheNewMystics.com/Ecstatic

Join live monthly web seminars at ***The Inner Sanctum***
www.TheNewMystics.TV

FREE WEEKLY TEACHING

Subscribe to *The Jesus Trip* ... a weekly video teaching on YouTube from John Crowder. You can join simply by visiting our web site: **www.TheNewMystics.com**. On our homepage, type in your email address and sign up for our weekly newsletter. You'll receive new video links every time they become available.

Or visit: **www.TheNewMystics.com/TheJesusTrip**

MORE BOOKS FROM JOHN CROWDER

The New Mystics
The supernatural generation

Two thousand years of miracle workers and pioneers crammed into one generation. The fiery bowls of Heaven are being poured out through an extreme body of spiritual forerunners. Are you called to walk among them?

Miracle Workers, Reformers and the New Mystics contains more than 70 photos, illustrations, and biographies of men and women whose lives have demonstrated the phenomenal throughout the ages. Let their stories inspire you to join their ranks as part of this revival generation. **$16 + Shipping**

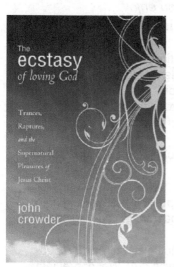

The Ecstasy of Loving God
Trances, raptures & the pleasures of Jesus Christ

God has destined you to live in the joyful radiance of Himself, just as Adam was called to live in the realm of Eden. Ecstasy, or "extasis," is the Greek term for trance, and is linked with a pleasurable, God-given state of out-of body experience recorded throughout the New Testament and the church age. In this book, John takes us on a journey from Old and New Testament ecstatic prophets to the future ecstatics who will usher in a massive wave of harvest Glory to the streets in these last days. **$20 + Shipping**

ORDER AT **WWW.THENEWMYSTICS.COM**
OR CALL TOLL-FREE **1-877-343-3245**

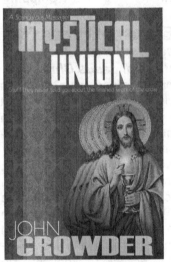

PARTNER WITH THE GLORY

When you invest in the poor, the broken and the lost, a tremendous oil of favor, finance and provision spill onto your own life and ministry. By working together to advance the kingdom, we are sharing the same harvest, reaping the same rewards and you are

connecting with the same anointing the Lord has placed on SOT. We value your support!

What your support accomplishes:
Housing, Feeding & Schooling Orphan Children
Massive Crusade Evangelism in the Nations
Equipping the Church through Media
Advancing the Gospel with Signs and Wonders

Join the Sons of Thunder Team!
If you have been blessed by the ministry of John & Lily Crowder and share our same goals and vision, please prayerfully consider becoming a monthly financial contributor. Simply visit us online:
Become a monthly partner at
www.TheNewMystics.com/Partners

OR CALL TOLL-FREE 1-877-343-3245

NOTES